BANDOOLA

BY

J. H. WILLIAMS

ILLUSTRATED BY
HENRY C. PITZ

LONDON 1955

READERS UNION
RUPERT HART-DAVIS

This RU edition was produced in 1955 for sale to its members only by Readers Union. Full details are obtainable from Readers Union Ltd at 38 William IV Street, Charing Cross, London WC2, and at Letchworth Garden City, Hertfordshire. The book is set in 12 pt Baskerville leaded and has been reprinted and bound at The Chaucer Press, Bungay, Suffolk, by Richard Clay & Co. Ltd. It was first published by Rupert Hart-Davis Ltd.

Scott.
Woodbourne.

BANDOOLA

TO
SUSAN

CONTENTS

FOREWORD

In *Elephant Bill* I wrote a little about Bandoola, that magnificent elephant, and his oozie Po Toke. I have chosen his name for the title of this, my second book, not because it is exclusively about him—it is not intended as the life story of an elephant—but because Bandoola was the most interesting and challenging animal with whom I have ever had to deal.

He and Po Toke were pioneers; before I had ever thought of going to Burma, they had already proved between them many of the theories which I was mistakenly given the credit for working out. Most of my work consisted merely in generalising what Po Toke had already done with Bandoola in his childhood and youth; and in order to explain this, I have tried to reconstruct this period in Bandoola's life from what Po Toke told me later.

But it is not merely for this reason that I have chosen to write about them. They were both most interesting characters, with great virtues and also with weaknesses which might have led them to disaster. Bandoola had an unfortunate reputation because he killed a man, but he was not a killer. Po Toke ended his life as a dacoit, or brigand. This was not natural development, but the

9

result of the peculiar conflict of his nature and his time. This conflict was already apparent when he christened the baby elephant Bandoola, after the great Burman patriot, General Maha Bandoola, whose reputation rested on his resistance to the British in 1824.

CHAPTER ONE
MAHA BANDOOLA

IN November 1897 Po Toke was an elephant-boy of fifteen. Fifteen may not seem a very great age; but the Burmese mature young. He had already picked the girl he wanted to marry, and he had chosen well. Ma Pyoo was beautiful and she was also the daughter of the contractor who owned the herd of elephants with whom he worked. Po Toke was one who aimed high because he had a justifiably high opinion of himself. He already knew more about elephants than any of the oozies of his own age, and more than most of the older men. He was ambitious, but it wasn't just ambition working in a vacuum. He was ambitious about elephants. Sometimes he told himself that he would know far more about elephants than the contractor himself. But that was a fancy he kept to himself. For the last year his thoughts had centred on his charge, Ma Shwe.

His suspicions of February 1896 had been confirmed. Ma Shwe was carrying a calf. Po Toke never knew who the sire was, but he suspected a wild tusker.

Wild elephants consider it the duty of the whole herd to protect an elephant carrying young, but in captivity the "auntie" system prevails. Instinctively they realise that to protect the young calf against the tiger two elephants are needed, and for a whole year before the birth the expectant mother and her auntie, Mee Tway, had grazed together and got to know one another in preparation for the great and dangerous occasion.

Every oozie is excited when his elephant calves; but Po Toke was especially excited. He was penniless, and he felt in some obscure way that his fortune was bound up with that of Ma Shwe's calf.

And yet there is nothing that an oozie, however thoughtful or ambitious, can do in preparation for the event, apart from keeping his animal in good condition. The choice of site is a matter for the mother and her "auntie." No tactful suggestions from outsiders are received.

Ma Shwe and Mee Tway chose well. They selected a spot where the creek made a crook-shaped bend. That meant they were protected on three sides by water, and it was silently running water. The least sound from the river could be heard. There were plentiful supplies of elephant grass, which meant good fodder. And in the centre was a gigantic Nyaung tree. The Nyaung tree is evergreen. Its roots penetrate so deeply that they sap the underground rivers of the jungle, and the Burmans say that under a scorching sun a Nyaung tree will give off a ton of water a day. The tree provided shade, and two natural buttresses protruding from its base made a bay like a natural stall.

When Po Toke left them browsing there at sundown, and walked down the track which the elephants had made in the seven-foot elephant grass, he had to admit that he couldn't have chosen a better place himself. There was fodder, shade, water and silence.

Overnight the mother and the auntie spent a considerable time circling the tree and stamping down the grass until they had flattened an area the size of a circus ring. The maternity ward was complete.

There was little fuss about the birth, though for half an hour there was great tension as Mee Tway went round and round the tree on guard. Then the sun rose and revealed to all the inquisitive eyes of the jungle—squirrels', birds', monkeys'—the tubbiest little male elephant calf ever born.

By the time that Po Toke arrived, the calf was tottering about timidly, as if uncertain where on earth he was. His trunk was just a deformity of a snout which he could scarcely move; and his small piggy eyes were surrounded with wrinkles, and as deep as those of an elephant over three score years and ten. On his little forehead and along his back were masses of long wavy hair in need of brushing. His toe-nails—five on each fore-foot and four on each hind-foot—looked as if they had just been manicured. His skin fitted snugly over his baby body, but it was serrated and loose at the folds, like baby clothes. His complexion was the kind of purple you get by mixing blue and pink in a paint-box. His little tail touched his hocks and persistent insects were already teaching him its use.

This is what Po Toke saw when he put his head through the grass. He called to the mother in a loud voice, and when she saw him Ma Shwe rumbled a sort of purr of pride. It was a pride which Po Toke shared; for this was his calf as well as hers. He came over and patted the calf, congratulated the mother and guided the little gaping mouth below the deformity of a trunk to the mother's teats between her forelegs. Mee Tway was grazing about twenty-five yards away. "Don't stray too far!" shouted Po Toke in a friendly way, and then left the maternity ward, whistling to himself.

He reached the sun-baked creek and began to move faster, hopping from boulder to boulder, repeating at first to himself "Atee! Atee!" ("A male! A male!"), rather as the proud father of an heir mutters to himself "A son! A son!" But as he got nearer to the camp, he raised his voice and he quickened his pace, shouting, "Atee! Atee! Atee!"

At first he was given a good welcome in the camp.

But as the day went on and he could talk about nothing but the baby calf and how wonderful it was, the older oozies started to make fun of him. "Are you sure it wasn't born with a golden tassel on its tail?" they asked. Perhaps it was really a white elephant, fit only for the palaces of kings.

At noon Po Toke picked up his spear and set off down-creek to visit his charges again. He was only just out of sight of camp when he heard the pattering of feet behind him on the jungle path. It was Ma Pyoo. As an unmarried girl, she wore her hair sadauk fashion in a page-boy bob with two symmetrical points curling behind her ears and forward to frame her cheeks. Her tamain or native skirt was tucked across above her breasts and fastened under her right armpit, leaving her shoulders bare.

"Po Toke," she said, "If you really love me as you say you do, promise that you will guard the baby elephant and promise that you will never let anyone ride him except my young brother San Oo, who is in the Monastery School at Yamethin."

Po Toke promised both these things. "If I accomplish this," he thought, "she will surely marry me."

He waved her good-bye and then hurried on, for this was something to tell his elephants as important as telling his friends of the birth of the calf.

As he approached the maternity ward, he called aloud to warn them of his coming. In answer came great elephantine rumblings to say that all was well with them.

He stayed with them during the afternoon. He kicked a recent dung-dropping from the mother with his bare foot, and as it broke apart, he bent down and looked at it. It was all right. Mother and newly-born were doing well.

Before he left them he gave to Ma Shwe and Mee Tway a ball of molasses each. He made another ball, spat in his hand and rubbed the ball in the saliva. That he gave to the calf to sniff so that it could learn his smell.

As the sun went down, the clearing seemed to be illuminated with a green eerie light. This was the time when some of the jungle-dwellers were thinking of their sleep and others stretching and licking paws and rubbing sleepy eyes awake. Po Toke knew that the coming night would be the most dangerous of all nights for his calf. As he went down to the creek on his way to camp, he saw that Ma Shwe had walked the fifty yards to the river to drink during his absence and Mee Tway had done likewise at another time. A good mother, a good auntie: they would not leave the calf unguarded. He was happier than he had ever been. He raised his voice and sang a Burmese love-song as he picked his way from boulder to boulder.

The elephants in their clearing heard his voice, so did a young full-grown tiger in a cane-break four hundred yards away across the stream. The tiger had chosen his lair with the same jungle instinct as the elephants had chosen their maternity ward, but with a different purpose. For days he had crossed and recrossed the track behind Ma Shwe. From the day an elephant's second milk falls into her udders, they leave a strong scent on all the leaves and branches that they touch. This scent had been an instinctive challenge to the tiger. He would kill and eat a baby elephant. It was his first attempt, but he knew that his best chance of doing so was within forty-eight hours of the calf's birth.

Even to approach his prey taxed all his jungle instinct. He knew that soon after sundown the breeze, however light it might be, would shift to downstream as the hot air rose from the valley. So he made his lair below the clearing, ready to work upstream against the breeze after crossing the river.

The tiger's lair was impenetrable. The tendrils of the creeping cane formed a tangled mass around and above it. He entered and left it by a tunnel which was scarcely visible. He had been there for several weeks, and he knew every track and cover-hiding for over a square mile round the camp. As it was the dry season he left no pug-marks in the creeks. He had even starved himself for the last few days, for hunger would increase his courage when the attack came. He knew the calf had been born by the rumbling sounds of pleasure made by the mother. He sat up and washed his face, as Po Toke went singing along the creek. The only sign of his excitement was the twitching of his tail.

In the camp there were fourteen men. Four of them were married and they had their wives and children in the camp with them. Married or single, they lived in bamboo huts with thatched roofs, on posts raised four feet above the ground. They were a hundred miles from the nearest jungle village. Yet they were happy and contented. The rice store was full and the jungle itself provided all the other things they needed for flavouring their curry.

That evening Po Toke was happier and more contented than any of them. He bathed in the stream. He tied his long hair in a knot and encircled it with a crimson piece of silk. He changed his daytime lungyi of indigo blue to one of vivid scarlet, and over his shoulders, which normally were bare, he put a coat of native cloth. He would have liked to wear a white one, but that was a privilege reserved for the elders of the camp: a sign of authority.

This was the Burmese courting-hour, and he had been invited by Ma Pyoo's mother to come to the bamboo veranda after the evening meal.

Ma Pyoo's toilet had taken her many hours longer. It had begun, in fact, as soon as she got back to camp after talking of the baby elephant and her young brother.

First she bathed in the creek. Then she put on a blue silk tamain skirt and a white coat starched in rice-water. On her feet she wore wooden-soled sandals fastened with a strap of crimson velvet. She smeared her skin lightly with thanaka, a cream made from rain-water and the powdered bark of a tree and scented with sandalwood. And finally in her shining bobbed hair above one ear she placed a bloom of the flame of the forest flower.

Po Toke ate with the bachelor oozies, squatting round a large bowl of rice. Ma Pyoo ate with her parents and her aunt in the privacy of their hut. A veranda ran along one side of the hut, and it was there the young oozie found her waiting for him, alone.

They talked about the future, as the young do who are in love but still too poor to marry. They talked of the elephant born that day, which Po Toke insisted would be an elephant of all elephants, and of how one day Po Toke, with Ma Pyoo as his wife, would own a camp of elephants like this one, and by then maybe this calf would be the prize of all his charges. Their love-making was very simple: holding hands and exchanging dreams of wealth and elephants and children and the day, which Po Toke said would surely come, when another General Bandoola would arise to bring freedom back to Burma.

When the time came to say good night, he did not kiss her; he just pinched her little toe and went down the bamboo steps. The camp was in darkness except for the glowing embers of the fires beneath the scattered huts. Most of the oozies had already gone to bed, but beneath his own hut a group of oozies was sitting silhouetted against the glow. One of them called him as he approached. "Po Toke, are there any bamboo torches ready, in case there's trouble to-night?"

"Torches?" said another. "He's too busy courting to bother about torches!"

There was a peal of laughter from the others, as Po Toke turned away towards the covered stand where the camp accessories were kept. There were two beings on earth he loved wholeheartedly, Ma Pyoo and this new-born elephant; and he could not bear either to be laughed at.

The stand was dark and filled with sacks of salt, molasses, grease for smearing harnesses, dragging-ropes, picks and axes. He felt his way towards where he knew the fire-torches were kept—bamboo sticks with one end steeped in resin, bound in bundles of six. There they were, dozens of new ones, prepared on the order of the contractor, while Po Toke had been out of camp. The oozies had known it all the time and they laughed when Po Toke came back and said he was going to sleep.

Before it was dark the tiger left his lair and crossed the creek a long way below the elephants' pitch. He worked stealthily upstream until his sensitive nostrils picked up the scent of the newborn calf being wafted down on the evening breeze. For some distance he boldly followed the open game-track along the bank of the creek. Then he re-entered the jungle, and for a time squatted motionless on his haunches, working himself up for the attack. There was more in this than hunger and a succulent meal; there was prowess. To attack two elephants and kill the calf would be an achievement worthy of the king of the Burmese jungle.

He could not decide in advance whether he would attack the mother or the auntie first. That would depend on how they were standing when he moved in to attack. But he knew that he could not seize the calf until he had stampeded both the adults. He must spring on the back of one and so lacerate her that she fled for safety; then he must unseat himself and stampede the other long enough to give him time to seize the precious calf and carry it off like a cat with a rat in its mouth.

But before he could attack, he knew that he must circle the clearing, because the best line of attack was from upstream. His patience was superb. Twice he moved up to within fifty yards of the clearing, but each time the breeze was coming downstream too fast for him to risk his scent being carried to them when he moved above.

The moon rose higher and higher, but it was not till well after midnight that the breeze dropped. Utter silence fell on the jungle, a silence so deathly that few human beings can endure it without making some sound or movement to reassure themselves. But the elephants made no sound. The two adults stood side by side, as unmoving as statues in the moonlight; and between the forelegs of his mother, with his little head just filling the gap, stood the baby calf, as motionless as they.

Occasionally the ears of the adult animals moved forward as if straining to hear a sound. Then Mee Tway broke the silence—for no reason—she just thumped the end of her trunk on the ground, and it rang hollowly with a metallic sound.

It eased the tension but it started the tiger on his first circuit round the clearing. He was fifty yards out, and he had decided to make his attack from the creek side. Four times he circled without crackling a leaf or a twig—the perfect hunter. He no longer walked with slow, stealthy step. He was now so near that at any moment he might see his quarry in the clearing. His poise was low on the ground. He moved forward with his powerful hind legs tensed under his body, ready instantly to spring. The tip of his tail quivered.

At last he saw the picture he had dreamed of: an elephant's flank clearly silhouetted, and only ten bounds and a leap away. His enormous power was released as he bounded forward and with a seven-foot spring landed on Mee Tway's back. His fore-paws dug deep into the barrel of the elephant's back. The vicious grip of the fore-claws held his weight, while with his hinder claws he lacerated the sides of the wretched elephant. With a murderous snarl he sank his teeth into the elephant's shoulder.

For a second Mee Tway was taken by surprise. Then bellowing with panic fear she was off, making for the nearest jungle, where she could shake this savage terror from her back.

As she reached the edge of the untrodden elephant grass she hesitated for a moment; and in that moment the tiger retracted his claws and slid off, as a child might slide from a bareback pony. Immediately he turned and bounded back to attack Ma Shwe, standing under the Nyaung tree with the buttresses of the tree protecting her flanks. She had the advantage of position. The tiger could only attack head on. He had no opportunity to manœuvre. She was terrified, but she stood her ground, with the calf huddled between her forelegs.

She took one chance. As the tiger checked before her, she took a pace forward and lashed at him with her trunk. With a lightning swing his right paw struck, the very movement of a cat at a terrier's face. The sharp claws struck home and Ma Shwe shrieked and bellowed with pain; for the trunk is the most sensitive and vital organ of the elephant. But she did not stampede. She replaced her off forward foot to protect the calf, who hadn't moved an inch.

But in that moment the tiger had gained his flank

position and sprang up on her withers. His fore-claws dug their hold and his hind-claws tore at her flesh. She rolled and shook herself to fling him off, but still she didn't stampede and still he clung and tore.

Her trunk hung limp. She had no means of touching her calf. The injury had made it quite numb and useless. She felt herself weakening. Was there no relief from this murderous weight?

Then suddenly it seemed as if the Nyaung tree had fallen on her. Something struck her with the force of an avalanche. She sank to her knees with the impact, without damaging the calf. And when she rose again, the murderous weight was gone. Mee Tway had returned, goaded to fury by her wounds, and charged at the tiger clinging to the mother's flank.

The king of the Burmese jungle fell to the ground. He was badly hurt in pride and body. But he managed to slide away back to his jungle lair.

Now the two defiant elephants stood side by side once more, the blood streaming from their wounds, but the calf stood perfect and untouched. They raised their heads and roared and trumpeted a challenge to all the tigers of the Ningyan Forest.

The only answer was the shouting of the oozies coming to the rescue.

Po Toke was still awake when Mee Tway broke the stillness with that first bellow as the tiger dug in his claws. He leapt up and in a moment the camp was in a tumult because despite their bantering all the oozies were asleep with one ear cocked and one eye open. In the moonlight figures were running to the accessory hut, shouting, "Mee Doke! Mee Doke! Mee Doke!" "Kya! Kya! Kya!" to get the bamboo fire-torches and scare off the tiger.

Now, with their spears in one hand and the torches in the other, they came hopping down the creek from boulder to boulder, as sure-footed as the wild goat of the mountains towering in the East. As he landed on a boulder, each oozie paused a moment to twist the ball and pad of his bare foot to dry it from the night dew, and in that moment of hesitation in their rapid progress the light of the torches shone on their copper skins. They had no fear of tigers, these men who were as much at home in the jungle as any animal. It was the tiger who had attacked the elephants who was afraid of the bounding torches and the yelling voices. For a moment he watched the fires dancing down the creek and then he slunk into the shadows of the jungle.

Po Toke was in the lead, calling down curses on the breed of tigers and yelling encouragement and words of love to his elephants to induce them to fight on.

They expected to find the worst when they entered the arena. For that reason they waited until they were all assembled and then advanced in a body holding their fire-torches high. But when they came to the

Nyaung tree, there stood Ma Shwe and Mee Tway side by side, rumbling alternate sounds of terror and delight. Ma Shwe was gurgling wet saliva in her throat, while Mee Tway beat the tip of her unwounded trunk upon the ground and made it ring like a blacksmith's anvil under the hammer.

Their ears were forward in excitement and fear. A sudden dread made Po Toke bend down and thrust his long-handled torch as near as he could without burning the mother's bleeding trunk. Between her legs he saw two tiny, frightened, piggy eyes. The calf was safe. He stood between his mother's forelegs, with his ears shaped like two little maps of India cocked forward, and above them the crown of his head appearing like a solar topee.

"Oh, Mother! He lives!" Po Toke yelled, and then, with joy in his heart welling up, he called to the little elephant. "Come out," he shouted; "come out, you brave warrior! Show yourself, Maha Bandoola!"

And so the little elephant was christened Bandoola, after the great Burmese general who had fought and died for the independence of his country.

No one ever thought of giving him another name. It was just as well. Because Po Toke, besides being a great oozie, was a great nationalist.

CHAPTER TWO

THE KIND SCHOOLMASTER

THE wounded elephants and the calf were taken to the camp immediately, so that the adults could have their wounds treated. But the calf Bandoola did not matter to anyone except Po Toke and Ma Pyoo. It had escaped from the tiger admittedly, but the contractor and the older men were agreed that that was only a postponement of its fate. It was certain to die one way or another; and a good thing too. Trying to rear elephant calves was a waste of money. It would be twenty years before it was any use in hauling timber. It was much cheaper and easier to capture young elephants from wild herds and train them by breaking their hearts and spirits.

Po Toke listened and he was too wise to argue. He believed that baby elephant calves born in domesticity would learn and work far better than any captured elephant. But he could only prove it by example—the example of Bandoola. So he relied not on logic but on love. In all his evenings on the veranda with Ma Pyoo he had spoken of the elephant calf, so that Ma Pyoo had almost come to believe that it was her own idea that her father should keep and train Bandoola.

It was fairly easy for Po Toke to persuade Ma Pyoo that he was right about Bandoola, because she was young and she loved him. It was not so easy for Ma Pyoo to persuade her father. He loved her, but he had known all that there was to know about elephants before she was born. If the calf survived the strain of the forest life when his mother was back at work, well and good, he answered.

Ma Pyoo bided her time. She was as clever and as ambitious as Po Toke, whose children she was determined to bear. She waited until her father went down with a worse attack of malaria than usual. Then, as she soothed his burning forehead with her cool hands, she whispered, "Will you give me Bandoola as a pet?"

"Yes," he groaned.

From that day onward no oozie dared to maltreat the calf. No oozie ventured to suggest that Bandoola was a nuisance. He became almost as important as Ma Pyoo herself. But though everybody knew that the contractor had given Bandoola to his favourite daughter, nobody, not even the contractor himself, knew that this favourite daughter had promised the baby elephant to Po Toke as soon as they were married.

Both the injured elephants responded to treatment. Mee Tway developed a sinus on her back which only permitted a light harness over the withers and across the breast. Ma Shwe's back healed completely, but she was left with a hole in the trunk where the tiger had clawed her. At first she found this very awkward when drinking. But she solved the difficulty by sealing the double orifice at the tip after sucking and then putting the side of her trunk against her mouth.

News passes fast in jungle camps and riverine villages. It was soon known that some wonder calf had been born and christened Bandoola after the great patriot. Some rumours even had it that Bandoola was a white elephant! Burmans on the move would ask to see this stalwart and the stories of his qualities grew in the telling. He was as thick as he was long and high. At four months old he had a dewlap and a wrinkled hide which could never gall. Under his tail was a bunch of loose flesh in the shape of a frog's head, and it hung so low that it provided certain protection from that blow of fighting tuskers which usually proves mortal. Between his fore-legs and back to his under-belly he had the point of perfection in the form of a loose bag of skin so aptly called a Pyia Swai or honeycomb. His eyebrows were straight above deep-set eyes, black as night and at first sight vicious, but on closer scrutiny kind, for their true colour was the equal of the pearl, with a pupil like a black bead. On his head he had black bristles stiff enough to prick the closest-tattoed behind, on his feet eighteen clean-cut toe-nails, ten fore, eight hind, and in the tuft of his tail four white hairs. Tusks could be felt in the cavities on either side of his trunk, and all were certain he would be a Tusker.

At four months he was so independent that he strayed well out of sight of his mother. He was so imitative that he aped his mother's every movement. When she squatted at the order Hmit, he tried to squat too; and at the order Tah he rolled over in play. He lay still in the water to be tickled when Ma Shwe was scrubbed, and they said that by the time he was five years old he would need no breaking. He would be one of the few calves born in captivity to equal any animal of the wild. Could anyone doubt that Ma Shwe had been mated by the Bwetgyi Monster, the great wild tusker of the Ningyan forest, to bring forth such a prodigious calf?

So ran the rumours. And they weren't without their foundation in fact. Some calves are nuisances, crowding at their mother's heels on the dragging-paths. But Bandoola kept clear and made the most the best days of his life, like a child, before being claimed for discipline and responsibility. Fun and mischief appealed to him; and he developed a trick in which he was encouraged by all the men and many of the women. The women wore skirts which were fastened by being tucked under at the hip, and unfastened, Bandoola discovered, by a gentle tug of his trunk.

To Ma Pyoo and the children in the camp he was a pet. He would pretend to have been left behind by his mother and then suddenly scuffle after her, wobbling like a tub. Everybody stopped and looked and laughed at him; and that was why he did it. But he also had the sort of accidents which all children have. He was stung by a bee. He slipped on the boulders in the creek. He split a toe-nail. He poked the tip of his trunk into a pot of hot oil. He walked on burning cinders which he thought were cold. These were the common accidents of childhood, human or elephantine, the sort of accidents which are part of education.

But there are with elephants, as with children, experiences which leave their mark in some fear or disability which lasts a lifetime. And Bandoola had one of these.

He was showing off how he could run and suddenly the ground gave under him. He had plunged into a swamp. His forelegs sank deep and the more he struggled, the deeper he went. His weight, which was remarkable for a calf of his age, was no longer a source of strength. It was his weakness. He rolled, he struggled, even more violently as panic possessed him; yet all he seemed to be doing was digging his own grave.

He sank until the cold mud lay beneath his tail at one end and his chin at the other. It held him like a vice. He was helpless. He couldn't even struggle any longer. The only sign of the effort he was still struggling to make was in his little piggy eyes turned skywards.

The largest tusker elephant in the camp was summoned, and ropes were made fast, not without protest, to Bandoola's tail and around his neck. Then the pulling started, and Bandoola was quite certain that his tail would be tugged from its roots and his head from his body before the mud would give him up. The Burmans knew better. They took no notice of his squealing. They urged the tusker on to pull harder, harder. And suddenly, with a pop like a champagne cork, out he came. But the tusker didn't let up; he went on pulling and bumping Bandoola until he was well away from the swamp.

This was an experience which, as I found later, Bandoola never forgot. And I have often wondered whether it was to be explained purely in terms of terror—the terror of finding that strength has become weakness. Was it also perhaps a matter of pride? He was showing off and suddenly his world gave way beneath him, and then, when he was hauled out, the tusker gave him the extra bumping to teach him a lesson. Elephants, like human beings, like playing the fool; but being made a fool of is a very different matter.

For five years Po Toke planned for the calf's training. Bandoola was to prove to others something of which Po

Toke was already convinced. But he was taking no
risks with his demonstration. Unknown to the contractor, Po Toke tried to keep Ma Shwe from dragging
heavy logs; and every day after she had finished work
he took her straight to good fodder before he attached
her fetters. The calf himself he won by stealing everything he could find as a tid-bit. By the time Bandoola
was five years old Po Toke could make him stand still
merely by gripping the point or lobe of his ear.

But to the others Bandoola was a handful. He found
that the other oozies were frightened if he chased them,
and he enjoyed stampeding them into their huts or up
a tree. It was all in fun, perhaps. But it was the sort
of fun which might end painfully and ruin the plans
which Po Toke had laid for Bandoola, and incidentally
for himself and Ma Pyoo.

His ambition was to train Bandoola by kindness
instead of by breaking his spirit. He went to Ma Pyoo's
father and asked for permission to arrange the training
in his own fashion. The contractor, like many an old
man faced with the challenge of youth, granted permission in such a way that if the experiment succeeded
he could claim some of the credit for it, and if it failed
he could say "I told you so".

Having been granted permission, Po Toke prayed to
the Nats—the jungle spirits—for guidance. A few days
later he found two shapely trees which grew so close
together that they would make a fine head for a crush

or pen. With the help of his camp-mates he drove in two uprights and fixed stout timber rails horizontally from them to the trees.

Then he asked for permission to visit the old Ponna, the astrologer, at the Shinbyuyan Monastery eighty miles away. The Ponna could cast the horoscope of Bandoola and tell him the time propitious for the beginning of his training. Po Toke was not quite certain whether he believed in astrology. But success was very important to him, and he was taking no chances.

He covered the eighty miles to the monastery in four days, and in gay clothes which he had borrowed he had his interview with the old Ponna. He gave all the information necessary. Bandoola had been born on the south side of the river. Po Toke guessed the hour of birth, but he knew that it was exactly five years and three months ago, and at the time Mercury was high in the sky and there was a full moon.

The old astrologer saw in the eyes of the young oozie the enthusiasm and love for his elephant. He kept Po Toke the whole day at the monastery, telling him stories of the elephant as a symbol of the Buddhist faith, and especially the white elephant. Buddha had entered the womb of Queen Maya in the form of a white elephant. The very river Irrawaddy which was the lifeline of Burma was called after Airawata, the Elephant of India. Not so very long ago all elephants were recognised as the property of the King.

Po Toke knew the story of Sinpyudaw, the last white elephant of the Royal palace of Mandalay, but he had never heard it first-hand from a great Ponna who had been to Mandalay and been granted an interview of worship.

As he listened to the old priest, Po Toke began to wonder whether his Bandoola was not a white elephant. He had only eighteen toe-nails compared with Sinpyudaw's twenty-two, it was true. But Bandoola had pale pink freckles on his trunk and cheek-bones, and when he came out of the river after bathing his hide had a pinkish glow. How wonderful, he thought, if his Bandoola became recognised as something extra-ordinary. There were no longer Kings of Burma in the Royal palaces of Mandalay, he knew. But might there not be a Burmese King again who would grant to Bandoola the royal privileges of the past?

Women would clamour to suckle him. A hundred soldiers would form his guard. Wherever he went, he would be attended by a Minister of State. He would live in a royal stockade and be fed on all the delicacies of the jungle and the field. He would bathe in scented sandal-water poured from vessels of gold. He would be trapped out in gold and silver and shaded by golden umbrellas. Dancing-girls would dance for his pleasure, and to send him to sleep would sing him lullabies.

The old Ponna told him all these things which he

had seen with his own eyes, and warned him to watch for every sign of the true white elephant as the calf grew up. His eighteen toe-nails were not important. It did not matter that he was not white in skin. Perhaps that mystic ring around the pupil, the pearl annulus, would grow. "Look out," the old priest said; "examine it each day."

With clear instructions as to the day and hour the training was to start and what offerings and rituals would be necessary to placate the jungle spirits, Po Toke returned to the camp. His heart was full of great things, and he had much to tell. The other oozies listened to him in silence and respect. He had grown in stature since five years ago they had laughed at his enthusiasm over the birth of Bandoola. Without fully realising it, he had developed authority. His certainty that he was right about Bandoola made him naturally a leader of oozies.

Bandoola was already ripe for training. For a calf of his age he was unusually independent of his mother. Ma Shwe's new oozie said that often when he went into the jungle to track and recapture the mother elephant for work, there was no sign of Bandoola. But he always returned to camp a few hours later, rolling in with a free, wobbling gait, like a guilty schoolboy who has been off on some exploit of his own.

When the day fixed for training came, Po Toke, the camp-followers and even the contractor himself, attended the ceremonial prayers to the jungle spirits at the base of the two trees.

At the head of the pen they had built a little shrine shaped like a Burmese doll's house, thatched with a grass roof. About it burned sixteen candles, one for each year of Bandoola's life to come before he could be considered a full-grown animal. His childhood days were over and the discipline of school years was about to start. Little cups of rice and cooked delicacies were placed in the doll's house to appease the hunger of the Nats.

The system of training captive elephants which I described as a routine in *Elephant Bill* was unknown until Po Toke devised it for the training of his beloved Bandoola. To give credit where it is due, Po Toke was the inventor and I merely the mass-applier of his technique. He greased the inside of the pen with fat from a roasted bear which had been speared to death by the camp men. Then on to a heavy branch protruding over the pen Po Toke fastened two jungle-made pulley-blocks. Through each he threaded a very pliable rope. At the end of one rope there were two nooses, through which San Oo, Ma Pyoo's thirteen-year-old brother, now home from school, could slip his legs. At the end of the other was a block of heavy ironwood. The pulling ends of both the ropes were tied to the side of the pen independently.

As the last candle spluttered and the flame died out,

there rose a scream of delight. The solemn ceremony was over, and everyone doubled back to camp and made a lightning change into working attire. Each man stripped to the waist and freed his legs by tucking his lungyi skirt up in front, passing it under the crutch and fastening the end in at the back of the waist. This combined the maximum liberty consistent with the modesty which is traditional to the Burman. It revealed also the full glory of their tattooing. For the naked Burmese oozie appears to wear skin-tight underwear from the knees up. Even the buttocks are covered with intricate patterns of animals and tracery. All of them wore their long hair tied in a knot. Though they talked a lot, they meant business.

Near the camp clearing Ma Shwe stood motionless, chained to a tree. Young Bandoola was loose, and very curious to know what all this commotion was about. He stood with his head towards the scene and ears well pricked forward, unaware as yet that he was to be the major actor in this little drama.

"Hok Thee! All right!" yelled Po Toke. He and the eight men under him ran to the training-pen. Ma Shwe's rider unfettered her, mounted, and began to follow them. Bandoola came behind, rather suspicious.

Ma Shwe's rider urged her to a fast gait and Bandoola doubled his pace to keep up to her heels. And so they reached the pen. Here they were showered with tamarind fruit and balls of cooked rice. The mother and the calf ate them with relish. Bit by bit, step by step, ball by ball, Bandoola was enticed nearer to the entrance of the pen.

San Oo was in position, silently dangling over the pen with his legs in the nooses. The contractor went into the pen and stood at its apex, holding out a whole bunch of bananas to Bandoola. Bandoola was interested, but suspicious. Life, he had found, was good, but never quite as good as that. He stood in front of his mother, but he made certain that his hindquarters were in touch with her trunk.

Bandoola knew there was some game afoot. He could sense it in the tension of the oozies standing round. He had attracted a lot of attention in his time, but usually when he had gone out of his way to seek it. This was different.

The contractor came towards him from the apex of the pen and offered him a banana. It was not a wild banana, but one of a luscious village bunch which Po Toke had brought back specially from Shinbyuyan. Bandoola tried to snatch the whole bunch from the contractor's arm. But the contractor dodged back towards the apex of the pen. Bandoola saw the man was caught in a trap, and followed up. The contractor was scared, apparently. He dropped the bananas and clambered over the side of the pen. Bandoola made to grab them and as he did so, he felt the pressure of his mother's head pushing his rump forward and holding him firmly in the pen.

Ma Shwe's oozie had received the signal and urged her forward. He held her tight while two oozies slipped two stout bars behind Bandoola's hind legs. And there he was in school—trapped. Ma Shwe, who had long lost interest in a son who had grown so independent of her, ate a few more balls of tamarind and went away without a sign.

Bandoola lunged out at the timber bars with his hind legs. The bars resounded but they didn't give an inch. He tried this way and he tried that, furious at the indignity of being trapped. But it was no use and he soon gave it up.

The moment he did so, a banana came through the bars of his prison. He took it. There was another, and another, and another.

San Oo, who was something of a clown, now began fooling about at the end of his rope. His antics were very funny. Everyone started to yell and roar with laughter. Men smacked each other's bottoms with delight. Everything was going wonderfully.

But then Bandoola tried his strength for the first time. He lunged out with one of his hind feet, and there was the sudden crack of splintering wood as he smashed the bottom bar. Immediately an oozie seized a spear to jab his foot back, but Po Toke yelled "No, no." He caught up a cane and yelled to the contractor, "Give

him more bananas," and to the oozies. "Quick, another bar!" Then he whipped the foot himself as the
new bar was fitted.

After the first half-hour Bandoola's efforts were less
powerful. Every now and again he would burst out in a
fit of temper, but every time he was calmed by bribes
of tid-bits passed to him through the bars. And these
tid-bits had been deliciously prepared. The tamarind
juice began to run down his jaws from the corners of his
mouth.

Elephants cannot sweat; if they could, Bandoola
would have been foaming. He must have felt in a
smaller degree the same sort of impotence he had felt
when he fell into the mud. He could not even steady
himself against the bars to get a purchase because the
bear-grease was now well smeared and his hide just
slithered against it.

Gradually the excitement died down. Bandoola stood
still. The chattering ceased. San Oo stopped his fooling. Then very slowly he was lowered into the position
of sitting on Bandoola's neck immediately behind the
wide and powerful young head.

The moment San Oo took his seat the storm began
again. Bandoola shook himself. That was no good.
Then he nearly stood on his head with his hind feet
resting on the top of the bar behind him. San Oo was
immediately raised, but Bandoola remained in this un-
dignified position resting for some minutes. The

moment he regained his normal position, down came San Oo on his neck. This time Bandoola stood on his hind legs and screamed with naughty temper. But San Oo did not care, because he was dangling on his rope up near the pulley-block, well out of reach.

Bandoola stood on his four legs again and immediately San Oo was sitting on his neck. This time the young elephant tried to reach him with his trunk and tear him off his rope. But a sharp rap from San Oo's cane on the tip of the trunk taught him better.

Then he swayed to one side, and very nearly did succeed in crushing San Oo's left leg between his body and the side of the pen. But not quite. Bandoola was beginning to learn that these men whom it had been such fun to send scampering into huts and climbing trees possessed a patience and determination which were more powerful than his brute strength. Without a let-up San Oo was lowered on to Bandoola's neck once every five minutes for about four hours. It seemed as if it would go on and on and on. For their will was stronger than his. He let San Oo sit his full weight on him and began to eat a whole stick of sugar-cane. San Oo sat for three whole minutes.

Then suddenly the indignity of the spectacle he presented returned to Bandoola, and he began to struggle once again. San Oo tried to control him but was forced to give the signal to be lifted up.

The next time San Oo was let down he was able to

sit on the elephant for half an hour. He detached himself from the sling, which was hauled up to a position in which he could grasp it if Bandoola gave more trouble. He did on several occasions, but each time with less determination. He was becoming reconciled.

The three men who had been raising and lowering San Oo now moved to the end of the rope suspending the heavy block of wood over the elephant's back. This was raised and lowered just as San Oo had been, but whenever the block was raised San Oo jumped on Bandoola's head. The object was first to show him that he could stand his rider's weight without discomfort, whereas the weight of the wood was intolerable; and then gradually to force the elephant to collapse into the position in which he pushed his forelegs out in front of him while his back-legs protruded out behind. The moment it was clear that this was going to happen, the elephant men started to chant, "Hmit! Hmit! Hmit! (Sit down!)."

At last Bandoola collapsed, with San Oo forgotten but not forgiven on his head, and the log now resting lightly on the middle of his back. Bandoola was looking frightened. His spirit had not been broken, but it was being firmly mastered.

After fifteen minutes the weight was lifted, but Bandoola made no effort to get up. The chanting began again, but with a new word of command. "Tah! Tah! Tah! (Get up!)."

He got up wearily, but immediately the voices changed to "Hmit! Hmit! Hmit!" and down came the weight once more; and down went Bandoola under it.

This went on for four hours, until he lost interest even in the bribes of sugar-cane proffered through the bars. He was performing his first movements under control almost without knowing it, he was so exhausted. And at last he could do no more. He sat down and he couldn't rise again. San Oo remained on his neck, now talking to him in sweet tones. The day was won. All the elephant men returned to camp except for San Oo and Po Toke.

It was evening before Bandoola rose again. He drank some water from a bucket, putting his trunk between the bars and then squirting the liquid into his mouth. He was cramped and he was tired—so tired that he did not notice when his forefeet were shackled with a hoop of cane.

The prison bars behind him were quietly withdrawn. It was some time before he realised that he was free to back out. Still riding him, San Oo helped him in his shuffling backwards by gently tapping him on the forehead with a cane.

Around his body, passing behind the withers and behind the elbows, they had fixed a circle of rope, which San Oo gripped with one hand. There was no certainty that Bandoola, once out of the pen, would not become a bucking bronco. He tried at first to struggle with his forefeet. But the cane hoop held him, and he developed a sort of long stride-hop in his journey to the tree to which his foot was to be chained for the night. Near the tree was stacked a mountain of bamboo fodder. Then he was left alone, to munch and meditate.

Later that evening Po Toke came down to see how he was faring and lit a large log-fire near him as company. As the pitch was within sight of the camp, Bandoola felt near home. Several times in the night he called his mother, a lonely, penitent call, as if to say that if she came to him, he would never stray again. But Ma Shwe did not come. From that night began his life as a draught elephant.

At dawn the whole camp visited him and Ma Pyoo brought him some cooked rice rolled into balls by her dainty hands. He didn't seem frightened that the ordeal of yesterday would be repeated. Po Toke placed his hand on his back and said "Hmit!" and he sat down at once, though when he gave the order "Tah!" the elephant did not respond for some minutes. Perhaps he remembered that infernal block of wood.

Po Toke and San Oo spent the whole day with him. San Oo was on and off the elephant's head continuously and by sundown Bandoola was completely under control. Po Toke had proved his method of training. An elephant could be mastered by patience and kindness. There was no mark or training scar upon Bandoola.

45

Even the contractor recognised and praised Po Toke's achievement. "Of course," he added, "Bandoola is a very clever elephant. And one must remember, it will be sixteen years before the beast begins to do any real work."

CHAPTER THREE

BANDOOLA COMES OF AGE

BANDOOLA was born at a time when dacoity or brigandage was rife throughout Burma. But by the time he was five years old it was rapidly dying out. Forest areas which had been the hide-outs of dacoits for years became safe again; and those of the British teak-trading firms which had managed to survive the troubles began to expand their activities. New leases were granted by the British Government easily enough in difficult and more inaccessible forest areas. The problem was that there weren't enough elephants. For years no wild elephants had been kheddared to replenish the captive herds, for one thing; and for another, hundreds of captive elephants had gone astray during the troubles and rejoined the wild herds.

In the meantime the contractors who owned elephant herds had doubled, and in some cases trebled, their prices; and when the question arose of working difficult forests, they flatly refused. If the teak trade was to be expanded, the companies who had leases on the forests had to build up elephant herds of their own. The old jungle salts who had survived the bad times were sent out through the forests to see what they could do.

One of these was a man called Bruce Walker. He belonged to an earlier generation, a generation which had sought consolation for the loneliness of the jungle in the arms of Burmese women. He was buying elephants for a British firm which had held forest leases under the Burmese Kings for many years, and had decided that in opening up the forests of the Upper Chindwin it would be better to employ its own elephants rather than depend on the caprices of extortionate contractors.

So it happened that one day in the year 1903, Bruce Walker and his attractive Burmese mistress came in search of elephants to the camp where Po Toke worked. Bruce had acquired in his youth a remarkable knowledge of the Burmese language by attending the monastery schools. He was familiar with the Buddhist religion, and at the period when all forest Europeans were liable to attack he had avoided the fate of many of his friends by sheltering in a monastery for six months under the protection of an old Burmese monk. He understood and liked the Burmese way of living and of doing business. So when in answer to his statement that he was

48

out to acquire a herd of a hundred elephants the contractor told him flatly that he had no elephants for sale but that he had an excellent five-year-old calf called Bandoola, Bruce Walker laughed and said that he was interested in no animal, male or female, under twenty or over forty. But he consented to look at the five-year-old all the same. The shortest distance between two points in Burma is never a straight line.

Po Toke for the contractor demonstrated the animal's points, how obedient he was, how magnificently developed and not a training scar upon him. "Yes, yes," Bruce agreed, "but, you see, we want to work these forests now, not in sixteen years' time." He was not impressed by the prodigious Bandoola, but he was impressed by Po Toke, who in his own way was equally prodigious. He was only twenty, but the manner in which he handled Bandoola showed that he had a way with elephants that was quite exceptional. The thought occurred to Bruce that, despite his youth, Po Toke might be the very man he needed as head elephant man or Sinoke to move his new herd of purchases up to Northern Burma. He asked the youth where he came from and found to his delight that he had been born in the Aya valley, a place to which some of the elephants would be going. "Come and see me this evening in my tent," said Bruce.

Before Po Toke arrived, Bruce had already discovered through Ma Win, his mistress, that Po Toke was a Kadu, a Shan gypsy tribe which had intermarried with the Burmans; that he had been to the Mingin Monastery School; that he was going one day to marry the contractor's daughter; that he had auza or deep respect from the other elephant men in the camp. It was an excellent report, and it decided Bruce to offer Po Toke the job of headman, despite his youth, at a wage which it would seem impossible for him to refuse.

But he did refuse; and being pressed, he said that nothing would separate him from Bandoola and he wanted to marry Ma Pyoo; and anyway perhaps the contractor would not give him permission to leave. He gave the impression that he considered himself as much the contractor's property as were Bandoola and Ma Pyoo.

It was an attitude that pleased Bruce, and he insisted that Po Toke should stay while he sent for the contractor. He might, even, despite his orders about elephant ages, consider buying Bandoola in order to secure Po Toke.

When the contractor arrived, Bruce told him nothing of what Po Toke had said to him or he had said to Po Toke. He merely asked how much the contractor wanted for Bandoola.

"I cannot sell Bandoola," answered the contractor. "He belongs to my daughter Ma Pyoo."

"In that case let us send for Ma Pyoo," said Bruce. "Perhaps she will sell Bandoola."

Ma Win, who was listening from inside his tent, immediately came out. She knew Bruce's weakness for young girls. "Is that necessary?" she asked. "Yes," Bruce said. "You go and fetch her."

While they waited for Ma Pyoo, Po Toke explained to the contractor what Bruce had suggested. He was excited. But the old contractor merely smiled, scarcely seeming to hear. He just squatted on his haunches and began drawing in the sand as if calculating the price for Bandoola. Po Toke, as soon as he had finished his explanation, stood up and was about to go, hoping to get a word in with Ma Pyoo before she arrived, but the contractor signed to him to sit down. Then he turned to Bruce and said, "I am an old man. Perhaps it is time for me to sell all my elephants and retire to the village where I was born. In that case Po Toke can do as he wishes, and the price for Bandoola can be the dowry for my daughter's marriage."

"And how much do you want for them?" asked Bruce.

The old man went through his elephants one by one, naming a figure for all, except Bandoola; and Bruce, knowing that in Burma these things are matters for careful bargaining, agreed that he would buy the elephants, but the exact price would be settled later.

Then Ma Pyoo arrived at the tent and made her shikos of obeisance to the Thakin, and her father told her that he had sold all his elephants, with the exception of Bandoola. Was she prepared to sell Bandoola, and if so how much would she want for him?

Ma Pyoo laughed. She was not yet sixteen years of age and very much a maiden. Looking at Po Toke, she explained that though her father had given her Bandoola, she had promised him to Po Toke when they married, so that she really could not sell him.

Then they all laughed, including Bruce, who now knew that he could save his face for buying a calf elephant by spreading his price proportionately over the prices of the other animals. He knew also that the old contractor would not be difficult in his bargaining, because this offer gave Po Toke the chance of becoming a well-paid Sinoke and marrying his daughter, who was now of age.

The price which Bruce agreed to pay the contractor for Bandoola was five hundred rupees, which made a satisfactory dowry for Ma Pyoo; of this amount he spread four hundred and fifty rupees among the nine grown elephants and wrote down Bandoola's price at fifty rupees, which made a satisfactory entry in Bruce's accounts. With Po Toke thrown in, he had got a bargain.

It took Po Toke six months to collect into one watershed all the elephants which Bruce had bought. In the meantime he was very happy. He had married Ma

Pyoo and together they were going to his home and friends in the Upper Chindwin forests. Only one thing slightly marred his happiness. While the contractor owned Bandoola, Po Toke could always fancy that the elephant was really his. But once the letter "C" was branded on Bandoola's rumps, he, like Po Toke, would be working for the company. If they were to keep together, Po Toke would need to use all his guile and ingenuity.

The march to the Upper Chindwin began in late September. There were a hundred and sixteen elephants in all and they departed in batches of seven to nine at intervals of three days. Po Toke and his wife led the first party, a group of nine elephants with Bandoola, harnessed with a miniature pannier and laden with some of Ma Pyoo's smaller chattels, wobbling along behind.

The last of the elephants did not arrive in the Upper Chindwin until April of the following year. On the journey two elephants died from natural causes, but there were no other casualties. The hazardous crossing of the Irrawaddy River was made on bamboo rafts without a hitch. Bruce congratulated himself on his choice of Po Toke as a headman, and he was so pleased with the condition in which Bandoola arrived at the end of the long journey that he gave instructions that the calf should join his six travelling pack-elephants.

This delighted Po Toke. San Oo was a splendid young oozie, but he wanted to keep an eye on Bandoola to see how he grew and developed. The calf had shown his ability during the journey, and every day he was with the pack-elephants he was learning something new, either by instinct when finding his fodder, which was at night more often than not, or from San Oo under Po Toke's instructions.

He was never punished cruelly. But he was corrected whenever he got up to mischief, such as squirting water over himself and half drowning San Oo when he was being bathed. So as not to scar his ankles he was given fetters made of cane. When he undid them with his trunk, he was put in chain-fetters for twelve hours, just to make him realise that his privilege carried with it a responsibility.

In the course of the eleven years he spent as a pack-animal he covered thousands of miles and visited every forest area in Upper Burma in every season of the year. Any attempt to use him for rice-transport was always foiled by Po Toke, who knew that there was a danger of galling his back through overloading.

At the age of fifteen his tusks began to take the shape which is called Swai Gah, after the posture of the Burmese dancing-girl, with arms bent upwards and out-wards. This gave him rather a wicked appearance when he raised his head and cocked his ears to look at any-thing. Those who did not know him were careful not to pass too close to him when they met him in the jungle, as he always looked as if he was about to charge.

By that age he was already as well developed as most young tuskers of twenty or over. And he had something which none of them possessed. His spirit had not, like theirs, been broken. His eyes were not cowed and his legs and flanks were unscarred. His lifting-power with his trunk or tusks was as great as theirs; but the obedience which he gave to his oozie sprang from trust and not from fear.

When Bruce saw how well Bandoola was shaping, he wanted to put him straight on to timber-work. It took all Po Toke's obstinacy to fob him off; and by the time that Bandoola was seventeen, even Po Toke had to agree that he should do harder work than transport, or there would be danger of his going on musth, and if he went on musth he would have to be chained up and would lose condition. But even so Po Toke and Bruce did not see eye to eye. Po Toke the naturalist thought of Bandoola in terms of the ages of man, Bruce the economist in terms of the wages of man. There was a strained difference between them, which ended in Po Toke's winning the concession that before Bandoola was put in dragging-harness he should be given a couple of years, pushing and lifting logs with his head, tusks and trunk.

So for two years Bandoola was sent to the Moo River among the old crock elephants, where logs stranded on sandbanks had continually to be rolled back into the main channel; a form of work reserved for pensioned tuskers, suffering from old age, deformities or incurable wounds that made them unfit for harness.

It was almost the last order which Bruce Walker ever gave. For war had broken out in Europe and, like many British Forest Assistants and Managers, Bruce Walker volunteered for service and was killed in action. Before he left he made Po Toke promise to carry out the extra responsibilities that would fall on him. How great those responsibilities were, Po Toke realised before he was very much older. For the duration of the war he took over practically the whole of Bruce's work of organising the timber-extraction, and during this time he had to leave Bandoola almost entirely to the care of San Oo.

The Spanish influenza epidemic, which swept the earth in 1918 and killed more people than the worst war in history up to that time, penetrated into the heart of the Burmese jungle in a form more virulent than was found in any city or village. Whole elephant-camps were riderless and work stopped for weeks on end, while the women, who for some reason had more resistance than the men, kept the herds intact by catching the elephants daily.

In the middle of this epidemic, word came to Po Toke that San Oo was dead. He liked his brother-in-law and was sorry he had died so young. But his first thought was for Bandoola. After thirteen years with San Oo how would Bandoola react to another oozie?

Picking the best man he had, he set out with him at once for the Moo River. The time had come, he decided, to move Bandoola to the Gangaw Forest and break him to his main task of hauling timber in the camp of Maung Aung Gyaw.

Bandoola had come of age; an elephant born, trained and bred in captivity, equal in strength to any wild elephant and unbroken in spirit and body.

Before he was transferred to the forest dragging-strength, Bandoola's descriptive roll was taken. Translated, this is how it reads.

Name	*Sex*	*Born*	*Mother*
Bandoola	Male	Nov. 1897	Ma Shwe

Height: 7 ft. 4 in.
Tusks: Swai Gah. *Right,* 2 ft. *Left,* 2 ft. o$\frac{1}{2}$ in.
Feet: Perfect. *Toes: Fore,* 10. *Hind,* 8.
Back: Banana Leaf.
Tail: To hock. *Brush:* Good, few white hairs.
Ears: Good, heavy-haired in orifice.
Skin: Loose and heavily corrugated.
Eyes: Pearly ring around parrot bead.
Brands: "C" on both rumps.
Identification Scars: Nil.
Remarks: Purchased from U. Ohn Ghine, Contractor, as trained calf, aged six. Trained by Maung Po Toke. Good temper.

CHAPTER FOUR

WILLIE AND MILLIE

DESPITE the difference in the lengths of their gestation, men and elephants have roughly the same
rate of development, the same span of life. Bandoola
and I were born in the same year; while I was at school,
he was receiving his education from Po Toke and San
Oo. Together we embarked on adult life. Bandoola, as
I have said, was a rare elephant in his generation, born
in captivity and educated to man's service not through
cruelty and the breaking of his spirit, but by the in-
domitable patience of Po Toke. He represented a new
generation of elephants.

In the same way the men who joined the firm of
Bombine after the First World War represented a new
generation of Forest Assistants. We approached life in
the Burmese jungle and the management of elephants
differently from our predecessors. We were ripe for the

58

ideas of Po Toke, which appeared to the senior men in Bombine as sentimental, unpractical, uneconomic.

But I am anticipating, for I did not meet Po Toke or Bandoola immediately I joined Bombine. In *Elephant Bill* I described my initiation into jungle life by Willie, my first forest manager. It was Willie who pronounced the dictum: "In this country there is the choice of two evils—women or the bottle. Choose which you like, but don't mix 'em." It was Willie who added, "Anything to do with the jungle, elephants or your work, you can only learn from experience. No one but a Burman can teach you."

Bruce Walker had chosen women. Willie had chosen the bottle. Though I would never have dared to mention it to Willie, it was my dream that one day in the distant future, when I myself was a Forest Manager, I should find a white woman who would share life in the jungle with me. Meanwhile I kept up an extensive correspondence with almost every girl I knew in England. "Damn lot of snippets!" Willie remarked, looking at my mail. "The only people worth writing to are your mother and your father." These, he hinted, should be written to alternately once every ten days. "Besides," he added, "think of the incoming mail. All these letters take up room. What about my cheroots? What about my whisky? What about my cheeses? The damn runner can't carry *everything*."

So letters were out and cheeses were in. And they

were, I admit, delicious cheeses. Willie would have them sent out specially from England, Wensleydales and Blue Cheshires, the date of their despatch carefully calculated so that they should not reach their prime before arrival. He knew how to treat a cheese to perfection, and he had it served dressed in a starched white napkin with all the pomp of a London club. It was one of the clues to the secret of his character, this effort to bring an English luxury into the Upper Burmese jungle. Though he was a real jungle salt, I feel that he had never become fully reconciled to being there, that his longing for his native country was constant and nagging, like an aching tooth.

After letter-writing was banned I looked round for some other hobby, anything which would serve as an excuse to get out of range of his sharp tongue. One evening I started to leave camp, when he called, "Where are you going, eh?"

"I thought I might find some birds' nests," I replied.

Had I said that I was going shrimping, he could not have looked more astonished. We were fifteen hundred miles from the nearest tidal river. "Look in the bamboo clumps," he said; "you might find a gannet's nest!" I laughed at his heavy irony, but he did not even smile.

An hour later I returned with six different kinds of eggs. He was astonished, though of course he wouldn't admit it. In all his forest service he had never seen six different kinds of birds' eggs. And to tell the truth, no more did I in all the remaining twenty-five years I spent in Burma.

It was a very tiny triumph, the sort of puerile victory which with any other person I would have forgotten, but not with Willie. He made everything a challenge, and though at first I thought it was just pure damn cussedness, I came to realise that it was his way of putting one on one's mettle. He inspired an almost vindictive loyalty, the desire to prove that one wasn't the fool he took one for.

I never got a chance to birds' nest again. "If you want something to do," he said, "we'll play cricket."

"And what shall we do for a pitch?" I asked, looking round the jungle.

"You make the pitch," he answered; "I'll provide the bat and ball. You ought to get a nice pitch ready by tea-time with the help of the oozies."

He sat back in his chair and slept his lunch off while I mustered a gang of elephant men, who should have been looking after their elephants, and set them to clearing the jungle, eradicating roots and stubble, watering it and stamping down the earth.

The more roots of shrubs and grass I pulled up, the more I despaired of ever getting a smooth patch to serve as a pitch. My oozies worked sullenly on in the blazing sunshine, plainly indicating that this was not their favourite form of insanity. Every now and again I would look across at Willie, placidly asleep in his chair. At last in desperation I went to my tent and removed the dhuri—a mat about six feet by four—from beside my camp bed, and pegged it to the ground with bamboo stakes. As I drove home the last stake, Willie woke up and went into his tent.

He came back with two cricket stumps. One of these he planted at one end of the mat, the other he handed to me. "These Burmans can't bat or bowl for toffee," he said, "but they're jolly good fielders." He placed them in a circle round the camp clearing, which wasn't fifty yards across and which contained our two tents. He set the field as if for rounders, and to Po Pyan, his loogalay or head servant he assigned the position of wicket-keeper, a position which from Po Pyan's expression of resigned disgust he had clearly occupied before. "You bat first," he said to me. "No scoring. No runs. Just bat." He took a grubby tennis ball from his pocket, paced out fifteen paces and made a mark, as if he was going to sling them at me like a demon bowler. "Play!" he called and made an action to bowl an underhand spin. Then suddenly he stopped. I had squared up, gripping the stump with both hands, batting as usual left-handed.

He stood with the backs of his hands on his hips. "What the hell do you think you're going to do, mow corn? Stand up and bat right-handed like a gentleman."

"I can't," I said; "I'm left-handed." I felt that if

only there had been another European in camp, I
would have been sent straight to bed.

Willie bowled a straight ball and I played it. The
second, an off-break, passed me and Po Pyan caught it
with a sigh. The next was a full toss, and I let fly for a
brilliant six. It was a satisfying sock. How many trees
and bamboos it hit before it came to rest I do not know.
But when at last it sank into the dense jungle, I turned
to smile at Willie; only to find him standing a couple of
yards away from me, his face purple with rage. "Do
you think tennis balls grow on trees, you idiot?" he
asked. "Or"—and here a horrible suspicion seemed to
cross his mind—"or don't you want *me* to have an
innings?" I could not have felt more shame if, on being
declared Out at the Oval, I had clubbed the umpire
over the head with my bat.

It was ten minutes before the ball was found, and
long before then I had reached the miserable conviction
that the least I could do to make amends was to get myself out. I need not have worried, because Willie's next
ball took my stump clean out of the ground.

"My innings!" Willie declared with an ominous note
of complacency in his voice. He took the stump and
surveyed the fielders.

I gave him a well-pitched spinner. He cut it, with a
twist of the wrist which amazed me, all along the carpet
of the jungle clearing to an oozie, who fielded it and
threw it in to me. The next he went forward to. It

came back to me like a rocket. He played every ball. He let nothing past him. With a straight stump and an eye like a hawk, he placed his shots all round the wicket.

After the first half-hour my thumb, fingers and wrist tired of spinning the ball. I lost all hope of bowling him by any fair means and I tried a fast sneak along the ground, calling out "Sorry" to cover myself as it left my hand. He just punched it straight back at me, without a word.

Cricket has never been my favourite game; but my fanatic loathing of it dates from that afternoon. When it had been going on so long that I felt I could scream, I called, "Do you mind if I increase the distance so I can bowl over arm?" It was the sort of little comfort which the damned, roasting in the everlasting bonfire, must get from turning over on the other side.

"No," he called. "Pitch them if you like."

Overarm was just what Willie wanted. It gave him balls rising higher, which he could cut with his powerful wrists. It was a joy to watch, I suppose; or would have been if I had been watching, lying back in a deck-chair with a cool drink in my hand. "Look out!" I shouted, "I'm going to pitch you one."

"All right," he answered; "I'll give you a catch."

A tennis ball has not the weight to be lethal, but my concentrated fury and frustration sent it whizzing so hard that I nearly dislocated my shoulder. Wham! He lashed it back at me like an ace service. I put out my hand—and dropped it.

I heard Willie say something.

"What was that?" I asked.

"Only 'butter-fingers'!" he said and nodded his head to a waiting servant to bring the tray with whisky and soda. He downed a stiff glassful in a gulp and as he saw me licking my lips, took up his stance and called out, "Play!"

I suddenly had an inspiration. "Hadn't these oozies better track and catch their elephants?" I said. "You remember you told me to check each evening or some would be missing in the morning."

"We draw stumps when I say, and we move camp when I say," Willie answered. "Play!"

So once again I reverted to off-spin, leg-spin, googlies, bumpers. It made no difference. My strength failed long before the light. "Pray God," I thought, "he never wants to start playing after breakfast."

At last he called, "Last ball!" If only he would take a final swipe and lose the wretched thing for ever! But no! A beautiful stroke, telling but restrained.

As the fielder returned it to him, he placed it in his pocket and said to me, "Remember to put this dhuri back in your tent. The night dew would spoil it, and it isn't yours."

Apart from having to bowl to Willie whenever I met

him during the next few months, I never played cricket again in my life. But I never told Willie with what abhorrence I regarded the game. In fact, when I met him my opening remark was, "Made any good runs lately?" It never raised a flicker of a smile. I didn't realise that these games were not in fact a private torment designed specially for my discomfort, but that Willie, who was a well-known bat in county cricket, was keeping his eye in for a tour with the Free Foresters when he returned to England on leave.

At last the rains came. "What a pity!" I said; "now we shan't be able to play any more cricket."

"No," he answered, "but we *can* play Northern Quoits."

I had noticed a young elephant whose sole task was the transport of an expensive-looking teak box which I imagined contained an armoury of big-game rifles. One afternoon, after several large whiskies, Willie thawed sufficiently to pass me the key of this box and told me to open it.

I opened the lid, having forgotten our earlier conversation about Northern Quoits. The top was covered with a yellow oiled cloth. When I folded this back there was revealed a complete steel discus set, a dozen of them decreasing in size, standing in a row, each with a slot to itself. I picked out the largest of them, a massive ring the size of a soup-plate, concave on one side and convex on the other. "What lovely burnished steel," I remarked, for want of something better to say. They were obviously old and as carefully oiled as a gun.

"D'you know what they are?" he snapped.

"Of course," I said; "a discus set. The Sikhs in India play them."

I would not have insulted him more if I had said they were tiddlywinks. "Put it back," he groaned. "Even Po Pyan knows better than that."

Four months of occasional meetings with Willie had taught me when and how to stand up to him. I replaced the discus, but left the lid open and went back to my chair. "Excuse me, sir," I said, "but what I said is right. The Sikh in full dress carries a light replica of that in his turban. The K.O.Y.L.I.'s may have been good marksmen, but a well-trained Sikh could sever even your tough neck at thirty yards with a throw and a spin. In fact he'd only have to say 'Shake your head' and it would fall off."

I laughed, hoping he would take the joke as I meant it. But he scowled. Then, removing the stump of a Burmese cheroot from his mouth, he said, "*What* did you call my regiment?"

I smiled back. I knew he had served with distinction not only with Kitchener's Horse in the South African War when he was a mere boy, but also in the 1914–18 war.

"The King's Own Yorkshire Light Infantry," I said deliberately. "And when next you want to mention what you've been in the habit of calling The Devons, it would oblige me if you would refer to them as The Devonshire Regiment."

He actually smiled; a smile of real friendliness. "Pass me one of the small quoits, will you?" he said.

Then he told me the game. On a piece of paper he drew an inner and an outer circle. Then, taking the discus, he explained the underhand action with a spin, the distance of the throw, the way it had to fall. It had to pitch within the rings, cutting into the ground with its sharp edge, and to count fully it had to remain standing. If it toppled over face downwards after the pitch, that is to say, with the convex side upwards, it counted half. But if it fell on its back, it was minus. "That's what we call a 'lady'," he added; "but you're too young to know why."

"Now get on and make a pitch ready," he said, "and if it's as good as your cricket pitches we'll have a good game; and by the way, we'll each need a couple of oozies as pickers-up."

I made the pitch, but I found it impossible to enlist any oozies for picking up. It was clear that, as well as Po Pyan, the oozies knew more about Northern Quoits. They vanished to a man in search of their elephants. I had to fall back on the servants, who received the news of this break in their routine with stolid apathy.

I asked Willie to throw first to show me how. He took the smallest first. It rose spinning from his hand;

at the top of its trajectory it flattened out and then as it fell, still spinning, it became vertical and struck the ground some twenty yards away with a plop. I ran to the target. It was upright in the inner.

Now I stood at the target end. The next was a bull. The third was also a bull. It scraped the edge of the second as it landed and stood almost as close to it as it had in the teak box.

The last and largest fell off in accuracy, but only two of them were lying down and both of those were face forwards. It was a joy to watch his action. He was even better at quoits than he was at cricket. I thought, but did not dare to tell him, that I would back him in any duel with a Sikh. Even the heavy one which had fallen short, I realised, had been placed deliberately so as not to displace the others.

Willie came up, and as he added up the score he described each lie, but beyond that he gave me no more instructions. "At least," I thought, as the servants carried the teak box back to the other end—"at least at this game we get an equal number of innings."

With my first throw I over-pitched the quoit into the jungle. The second very nearly decapitated the servant who had gone to find the first. "Look out," bellowed Willie to the Burman and, turning to me, purple with rage, he said, "You . . . you . . . you Sikh."

My length improved but not my angle of incidence. Only one was standing in the target, a lucky inner.

Having thrown the last one, I ran to the target, an error of taste I realised, remembering how Willie had strolled up. "Well?" asked Willie.

I looked down. "I'm only twenty-three," I said, "and I don't mind admitting I've never seen so many ladies lying on their backs."

"Nor have I," said Willie, laughing, "and I'm over fifty."

This I remember as a very important afternoon, because in it I had made Willie smile once and laugh once. It was the beginning of the thawing process, almost as gradual as the melting of the polar ice-cap, but at least a start. And as I got better at the game, so Willie in his unbending way unbent.

During this trip I had an unpleasant task when we visited Po Toke's camp. I had already conceived an admiration for Po Toke, but one of the questions on which we could never see eye to eye was the medical treatment of the animals. Po Toke, who believed in faith, had allowed an enormous abscess on the chest of one of his tuskers to go untreated. This he had at first hidden from me because he was ashamed. We both of us awaited Willie's inspection with trepidation.

The best method of defence is attack, and when we came to this tusker, I went in front of Willie to the elephant's head. Out of the corner of my eye I could see Willie, saying nothing, but with an expression on his face which showed that at the very sight of the abscess his cheroot had turned damp and bitter in his mouth.

I tapped the tusker under his lower jaw and the animal raised his head with his tusks resting almost on my topee. I felt the abscess. It was twice the size of my fist. I looked back at Willie, expecting some comment, perhaps even a word of advice. But he said nothing; he just looked sick.

"It's as ripe as a tomato," I said. "I think I'll open it up now."

He made no comment, moving away as I thought in disgust, and went over to a log and sat down.

"This is my hour," I thought, and turning to Po Toke I asked him in Burmese for a knife. Po Toke drew from a sheath on his hip an ivory-handled dagger. Seeing it, the rider bent down and said something to the tusker which I did not understand but which I took to mean, Now behave yourself.

I stabbed the abscess with the dagger, and the pus poured down the animal's chest and foreleg in a stream. I cleaned the abscess out with my fingers, then syringed it with a dilute disinfectant, which I also used for washing the animal's leg and my own hands and forearm.

The whole thing took about five minutes. "Well," I said, much relieved, "I think that's that, sir." It was a nice job, and I considered that if I had not earned any praise, at least I had avoided a rocket.

71

Willie got up and remarking rather grimly, "We'll talk about it later," he continued his inspection. He said this as much to me as he did to Po Toke, and when, after Willie had taken his first whisky of the evening, Po Toke appeared and fell on his knees, I felt that the least I could do was to kneel beside him.

Willie turned to me. "Didn't this headman tell you that animal was dangerous?"

"No," I said; "but in that case why isn't it down in the inspection book?"

"It is," he answered, "as you'd know if you'd taken some trouble to learn to read Burmese. It's a wonder the animal didn't knock your block off."

"Well, why didn't one of you stop me operating?"

"For precisely the same reason that the animal *didn't* knock your block off," Willie said in a tone which, despite the ambiguity of the words, made me feel that this was the kindest, the most human thing he had said to me in six months.

Then he began speaking to Po Toke in Burmese. He was far too fluent for me to follow, but though he never raised his voice every word he said seemed to go home like a blow to the body. When Po Toke left, he looked shaken and resentful. I wondered if Willie had given him the sack.

Willie took another drink and then he said to me, "You've got to watch out for Po Toke. He knows a lot about elephants. But he's not a Bombine boy. We bought him with that elephant Bandoola. He's very good, but there's something I can't quite trust. Watch him as you go on."

It was the first hint I had received that I would have the chance to "go on." In a few months my probation year would be over and my future depended on Willie's report.

But Willie was going home on leave at the end of my probation year. I felt that even if his report were favourable, I should think twice about going on, if Willie's successor was likely to take such a long time to thaw out as Willie had.

During the rainy season I had three attacks of malaria. Though I had been used to that during the war, I never got a more welcome letter than Willie's note to say it was time that I came out of the jungle for a change. He met me on the main river, and we had one night together before we boarded the steamer for the three-day trip to headquarters.

I had not seen him for three months. I think that he was rather shocked at my appearance, because the fever had been severe. He was so pleasant that I almost felt that he would have given me six innings to his one.

"By the way," he said, "you've got an overdraft and I've been told to say the Company is worried about it."

"I'm even more worried about it," I answered, not adding that it had piled up through keeping pace with his thirst.

"I'm glad to hear that," he said. "I'm not against a man drinking, provided he can afford to."

Then he told me that I was not only confirmed in my appointment, but I was to take over a large district to relieve a Senior Assistant, Rasher. "Your new Forest Manager will be Millie," he said. "You may think that I've been an absolute devil this last year. You're quite right, I have deliberately. You'll find Millie a much nicer man than I am, but I trust you to serve him just as loyally all the same."

There was no chance to consider refusing to remain. That night I found myself at last accepted, and the acceptance was all the dearer because it had been so hard to win. I went to bed in a state of simple exaltation, the sort which a boy feels the night after he has won his school colours. But I did not sleep until a malarial ague had sweated a few more ounces off me.

I was bitterly disappointed to find when we went aboard the river steamer that there were other passengers. For the first time I wanted to travel with Willie alone, so of course it would happen that there was company.

The skipper we already knew, a type who had reached the terminus of thirst, Crême de Menthe frappé. The engineer was still playing the same gramophone record with an affection which apparently grew even deeper as the grooves were more worn. The name on the label was "Banana Oil."

These men I was expecting, but in addition there were an American oil-driller who was as tough as hell, his cockney assistant, a miserable little man who gave the impression of having been born poor and having stayed poor all his life, poor in pocket and poor in spirit, and lastly there was a missionary, a meek and gentle creature.

Our cabins surrounded a small furnace which was dignified by the name of The Saloon. As if it wasn't already stifling enough, the American oil-driller raised the temperature even higher by emitting a stream of blasphemous obscenities whenever he opened his mouth. These, uttered at close quarters yet almost without interrupting the mastication of chewing-gum, caused the missionary acute embarrassment. I myself was more infuriated by another habit of his. He was a superb diver and whenever we tied up at a river-stop he would give a display from the captain's bridge, which was a good twenty feet above the water-level. For me the effect was marred by his flinging his unfortunate bull-terrier bitch in first and laughing to see her belly-flop. When I told him what I thought about it, there was almost a row, until Willie placed a double brandy in his hand and called him Jake. It is a peculiarity I have noticed about people called Jake and Hank; they never feel really happy unless someone, no matter if it's a complete stranger, is calling them by their Christian name.

After dinner Jake wanted to play poker. Our eyes all turned to the missionary. "I don't know how to play," he said, "but I'm game to learn on condition you'll moderate your language for the rest of the evening, Jake."

This offer, combined with the use of Jake, completely won the oil-driller's heart. "O.K., Mister Sky Pilot, it's a deal. Goddam it if I'll swear again to-night."

Banana Oil and Crême de Menthe frappé excused themselves on the ground that they would have to be under way at dawn. The saloon table was cleared and Willie suggested that instead of poker, we should play Northern Farmer, which is much the same but rather simpler.

We played for a couple of hours. The missionary, with beginner's luck, held wonderful cards and played them shrewdly. The American, deprived of his freedom of speech, was slightly down and so was I. I remembered what Willie had said the night before about my overdraft, and knowing that I could ill afford to lose any money I played hesitantly, which is a fatal thing.

When it came to the last round, however, we were all a little reckless. The pool built up until it contained about seven hundred and fifty rupees (fifty pounds, which in those days was a lot of money). By that time there were only two of us left in, the cockney oil-man and myself. It was my turn, and I had a five of spades. If I chucked my hand in, the cockney would clear the pool. If I called him and won, I would share the pool; but if I lost, I would have had to pay in another seven hundred and fifty rupees, which I hadn't got.

My card lay face down on the table. I looked at the cockney. He had on his face an asinine smirk. He was sitting pretty. He had everything to win and comparatively little to lose. At such moments, when a gambler is playing for stakes higher than he can afford, a curious empty feeling assails him—or at least it did me. I felt that I was incapable of making a correct decision. I looked at the American, but his interest had gone the moment he flung in his own hand. The missionary was watching with a sort of shocked fascination. This was exactly the reason why he disapproved of gambling. I turned to Willie.

To any of the others Willie's face would have appeared expressionless. But I, who had studied it over the past year for the slightest variation of mood, could read as plainly as anything the gathering disgust at my hesitation. He might as well have said outright: "Don't worry about the money. I'll back you for fifty pounds or five hundred if need be. But if you don't call him, I'll never speak to you again."

"All right," I said, as much to Willie as the cockney, "I'll see you" and I turned up my five of spades.

"You sure?" said the cockney.

"I'm sure."

The cockney turned over his card. It was a four.

At 6 a.m. the next morning I was awakened by a cool hand on my forehead. I opened my eyes. Willie had a glass in his hand. "Drink that!" he said. "Champagne and stout. Do you a world of good."

It was the last order he gave me as my No. 1, and I obeyed it willingly and then went back to sleep.

I saw him a few times before he departed on leave. From somewhere in England I received a laconic postcard. "How goes the cricket? I got a century yesterday. Keep fit." I was in camp with my new Forest Manager Millie when it arrived. I passed it to him. "Isn't that typical?" I said. "You may not realise it," Millie said, "you've only known Willie for a year, and I've known him for twenty. You've been very highly honoured."

Millie was a complete contrast to Willie, a man of the most gentle disposition. He was a strange man to find in the jungle, because a study would have been his spiritual home. For him no cricket, no quoits; at every opportunity he retired to read a book. He had little feeling for animals. He never kept a dog and seldom came very near to his elephants. He never criticised any of my work; he seemed to take it for granted that I knew as much as he did. It was his method of teaching, because it forced me to pick up his knowledge by attention.

This may sound as if he was inefficient. He was not.

But he was by nature a reader, a student. He was not apparently interested in the inspection of elephants. But their droppings he would read most studiously. He could recognise these more easily than he could the elephants heads. Every elephant-dropping he came across in a working area he would examine, prodding it with his shooting-stick. Usually he had no comment to make, but occasionally he would say, "Look at that. Mee Too's been eating earth again. I don't like that." Prod, prod. "Um. Elephant-worms again." Or, "Poor old Kah Gyis. Beginning to show his age. Bamboos passing through him like tough string." (I can never speak or write of Millie without seeing him in front of me on the march with two inches of his white underpants showing below his blue shorts.)

It was not until Millie's digestion gave out too, and he went sick for a long period, that I appreciated he knew four hundred elephants in that forest by their digestions. He never did very much about them except to tell the oozie in a bashful way. But it whetted my observation for the next quarter of a century; and henceforward one of my precepts of elephant-management became, "By their droppings ye shall know them."

CHAPTER FIVE

BANDOOLA ON MUSTH

BANDOOLA and I did not meet till we were twenty-three; and Po Toke, who introduced us, made the most of the fact that we were the same age and both embarking on our adult life in the jungle. He felt this very strongly, but I have no doubt that even if he had not felt it, he would have used the argument in order to induce me to show sympathy towards his favourite. There was in Po Toke's feeling for that elephant almost the passionate desire of a father to help and protect his son. It might have lessened, I think, if Ma Pyoo had been able to give him a son of his own; but after eighteen years of marriage she was still childless and so his paternal pride and love were lavished on Bandoola.

Every Forest Assistant claims to have managed Bandoola at some time in his career; for to inspect him and have him in one's herd produced a feeling of pride.

I don't know how many of them felt as I did, in addition to this pride, a feeling of understanding him as a fellow-creature closer than many human beings. It was not merely that chance or fortune brought me together with him and Po Toke off and on during the next twenty-five years; it was also right from the start the sense that Bandoola and I, being of the same age and living in the same jungle, were facing very similar problems. And of course Po Toke did his best to instil in me a sense of responsibility towards the first product of his training methods.

Po Toke, as I have said, had been a pioneer of the theory that calves born and trained in captivity were far more suitable for perpetuating the elephant herds than the wild elephants kheddared and broken in spirit. I was impressed by the logic of his arguments and completely converted to his views. And so were a number of forest managers and assistants. More and more of them came to regard the pre-natal care of a prospective mother-elephant as important. Remarks in elephant-inspection books read: "Expected to calve November; rest from work all October and three months following birth of calf." The times were changing.

But individual training did not prove a success. There were only one or two oozies with any outstanding gift for training; none with the genius of Po Toke: and no trained calf ever developed in the same prodigious way as Bandoola. The decision was taken to start a number of training-camps with a school of young elephants in each, and Po Toke was appointed general trainer.

In a sense it was a triumph for him. His theories and methods had been officially accepted. But it meant that he could no longer keep an eye upon Bandoola, and with San Oo dead he got no news of him from the oozie. That was why Po Toke appealed to me.

I was so convinced of the rightness of Po Toke's methods that I made every effort to see that during Bandoola's early years of dragging timber he was not overworked. But the Senior Timber Assistant immediately above me had very different ideas. He was a man called Rasher, nearing the end of his time and violently opposed to the new-fangled methods of elephant-training which I and others of my contemporaries regarded as plain common sense. Bandoola became the symbol of our difference. I would place him in a camp where timber was small and the forest easy to work. Rasher on his next term of inspection would move him back to heavy timber and the stiffest precipitous country.

When we periodically met, we thrashed our arguments out in camp over whisky; for Rasher, like Willie, was married to the bottle. "You're crazy," he said. "Just because an elephant lives roughly as long as a man, you sentimentalise him and pretend that he has the feelings, the temperament, the character of a man. I've heard a lot of nonsense in my life, but never such un-mitigated nonsense as all that."

I felt at a loss in answering, because the truth was that Rasher himself was nearly crazy. Desperately lonely, he lived close to the cracking-point. Alcohol was the only thing which gave him the energy to carry on. He was tough and hard on animals, but he could say with truth that he drove them no harder than he drove himself. The only way I could have proved my argument would have been to break through his tough-ness to that soft centre underneath; and if I had suc-ceeded, it would have broken him even quicker than alcohol was doing. He had the frantic will-power of the alcoholic.

It was a Goanese doctor in a small up-country station who took me on one side and warned me that if Rasher was to get home on his next leave in three months, I should have to remain his constant com-panion in the jungle until it was time for him to go out.

The prospect terrified me, as only those who have lived in the jungle can appreciate. Even living there with one's greatest friends makes one want to scream at times. But Rasher and I had nothing in common. My interest in elephants was young and intense. His had disappeared years before, and nothing had taken its place except the bottle. He carried a flask of whisky in his pocket, and before beginning a climb from one watershed to another, a climb of perhaps two thousand feet, he would prime himself with half a flask. When he reached the top he would pause and celebrate the victory with another deep pull. That would give him the energy to flounder down the other side, but when he reached the next creek he would need another pull.

He frightened me, I don't mind admitting; because there had been a time when he had been as interested in the jungle life as I was. Looking at him, red-faced and jittery, I had a nasty premonition that I might be looking at myself a quarter of a century older. "Women or whisky," Willie had said. The idea of taking a Burmese mistress as Bruce Walker had done did not attract me; and though I liked drinking, I was horrified by the later stages of these marriages to the bottle. I loved the life, but I wanted a woman of my own race who would share it with me. But what woman in her senses would?

I thought of these things, while I encouraged Rasher to pickle himself as soon as possible after sundown. It was the only way to ensure that he got his rest. From morning to night he smoked Turkish cigarettes made in Greece; and even when I got him into bed, he would pick up a book and light a cigarette, making the last pretence at sobriety. Suspended from a string inside his mosquito-net he kept an empty cigarette-tin in which there was a little water. I would hear him strike a match and puff at a cigarette, trying to focus on the printed page. Then after a very little while, the book fell forward on his chest and with a sizz the cigarette dropped into the water. "Sizz" I came to think of as the way he said "Good night."

In the three months we were together, he only missed the ash-tray twice. Luckily on each occasion we were sharing the veranda of a hut and I noticed before I fell asleep that his mosquito-net was on fire.

I racked my brains for something which might give Rasher some new interest in life, and I found it in my camera. He had never done any photography and he grew interested in a set of photographs I was trying to build up of game-tracks. He wanted to try his hand, and to encourage him I ordered him a complete photographic outfit, including developers and printers.

It was wonderful the change that came over him. He wanted to photograph elephants; his enthusiasm suddenly revived as he realised that instead of seeing them every wretched day of his life he would soon see them only in zoos and at circuses. He promised to take a photograph of Bandoola for me and he cut down his drinking because it hindered his hobby.

One evening we agreed to do some flashlight printing as soon as we had had some food. We rigged up my tent as a temporary dark room. We set up the table and laid out the equipment: the red developing lamp which smoked malodorously, the trays of liquids, developers, fixers and washes, and spare glasses of all the necessities.

Before we started, Rasher was by his standards cold stone sober. But he fixed himself an extra large whisky-and-water and placed it on the table before him, when we had taken up our respective positions. I was to fire the magnesium pistol, while he held the printing frame.

"Right ho! Lights out."

Except for the glow of the developing lamp we were in darkness. I fired the pistol. He took the print out of the frame and placed it in the developing bath. Then he fixed another print.

Everything went well for a time. He worked with the enthusiasm of a boy absorbed in a hobby. And then the urge to drink came back to him. "Wait a minute," he said. He was as impatient as I was to get on. He picked up his drink and drained it down in one.

Then he sprang up, spilling liquid from the plates and knocking over glasses as he staggered to the tent-flaps. Everything was ruined. "What the hell's the matter?" I asked, furious.

"I've drunk the bloody hypo," he groaned and then collapsed.

For a week he did not smoke or drink whisky. The glass of hypo combined the effects of Epsom salts and mustard water. After that, Rasher's passion for photography vanished. "Pure waste of time," he said.

86

But though he went back to the bottle, his system had been so thoroughly flushed that it couldn't build up its poisons again before his home leave came.

The Goanese doctor congratulated me, when I saw him next. "You did a wonderful job," he said.

"It wasn't me," I answered. "It was the hypo."

Rasher never came back to Burma. He knew it was the end. He had fifteen thousand pounds in capital, the savings of a life-time; and three years, he reckoned, in which to spend it. They say he spent six months of every year in a nursing home for repairs and maintenance, and the other six months over-lubricating the works.

When he died at the end of the three years, his whole estate, amounting to one hundred and fifty-eight pounds, was bequeathed to the R.S.P.C.A.

When I joined him, Rasher was beyond writing, and never kept a note. He had a rusty typewriter, every letter-key of which was indecipherable because it had been obliterated by the stubbing out of cigarettes. He could type a letter slowly, looking down at the type-faces when he was in doubt which letter he wanted, but the signature of the letter was an agony. His trembling hand would remain poised holding the pen above the paper for minutes. Then with a stab he would strike the nib deep into the paper and having obtained a grip he would carry it across the paper with a long determined wobble, not a letter of which was legible.

And yet Rasher was a man who knew a great deal about elephants. I often wished in later years I had pressed him harder to obtain his knowledge. But I doubt if I should have got it, even so. His early enthusiasms were stone dead.

There is one thing I remember that he told me; that the Dance Halls described in *Toomai and the Elephants* were figments of Kipling's imagination. The dance hall he had been told of was really the maternity ward of a herd of wild elephants, which prepares for and guards the new-born calf in much the same way as Ma Shwe and Mee Tway prepared for and guarded Bandoola, except that the whole herd is involved.

After Rasher left, I saw Bandoola every month or six weeks. As far as the disposition of my elephants was concerned, I was now my own master; or at least I was supposed to be. But I learnt very soon that in the jungle a man is never completely his own master, far less the master of his elephants. It seemed to me that the real master was the monsoon, and his innumerable servants were the leeches and the malarial mosquitoes. And against these forces the only defence lay not in alcohol but in keeping fit in mind and body.

Not long after Rasher went home, a man came to my camp and asked to see me. I knew him. He was an opium-addict, who lived in the jungle camps like a roving gypsy and who made his livelihood out of peddling opium. He told me that he had come from the camp of Maung Aung Gyaw. I asked him how things were going there. They were not going well, he answered, not at all well.

After that I gave him no help. I knew that he had come to get something for himself, and in time he would come round to it. He began by abusing Maung Aung Gyaw himself as incompetent to run a camp and then he started on Bandoola's oozie, who was useless.

"In what way is he useless?" I asked.

"Bandoola is on his first musth," he answered. "The oozie cannot recapture him. The whole camp is terrorised. Bandoola is dangerous. There is no telling what he may not do." He went on to tell me what *I* should do: dismiss Maung Aung Gyaw and the oozie, for one thing, and for another offer a reward for Bandoola's recapture; a reward which I fancied my informant hoped he would collect himself.

But I did neither of these things. I merely said that I would visit the camp myself, having no idea what I should do when I got there. All I knew was that I wanted to learn something about musth at first hand.

I had sat near camp fires and listened to old Burmans giving their ideas about it, as though it was a form of madness or possession. I had argued about it with other jungle men. But I had always felt myself on weak ground because I had never seen an animal on musth. For all that, I was convinced that there was nothing

abnormal about musth, unless the sexual urge was to be
considered abnormal.

When I reached Maung Aung Gyaw's camp, Bandoola had been lost for five days. If the informer had
lied about everything else, he had at least told the truth
about the panic. All the elephants in camp were
chained to trees as a precaution against the demon
Bandoola ranging at large on musth.

I had brought with me Kya Sine, my hunter, who
was later killed by Poo Ban. Together we set out to
track Bandoola. Kya Sine led and I carried a shotgun
only, as I was not hunting him. We followed his tracks
by the old spoor to about five miles from the camp.
There were no fresh spoor or droppings to give us any
indication that we were near him. (Perhaps elephants
on musth are constipated, I remember thinking.) What
showed us we were near him was the bleeding bark
of the trees which he had been stabbing with his sharp
tusks.

As soon as we saw them, we cut away from his tracks
and went down to the river-bed, which just there was a
mass of huge granite boulders, round which there
flowed a silent trickle of water. It was a sweltering hot
afternoon in April. I was sure Bandoola was nearby.
I could feel his presence. I could visualise him standing
perfectly still, waiting to charge us.

I told Kya Sine to sit in the shade of one of the huge
boulders, placed everything I carried beside him and

told him to wait until I came back. Then I began to work upstream. I was wearing rope-soled shoes, which were almost as silent as Bandoola's own feet. But there was not a sound. I had been gone about an hour when, looking over a huge boulder, I suddenly saw him.

He was not the Bandoola who had been described to me, stark staring mad on musth. He was the same Bandoola I had always known. He was down in the creek, standing under the shade of an overhanging tree. For a moment I thought that he was facing another elephant, but then I saw it was a boulder about his own size.

He seemed to be making some sort of obeisance to this boulder. His trunk swung from side to side in the movement which the Burmans call rocking the cradle. And when this stopped he rocked his body from side to side, standing on alternate feet in the movement described as winnowing the rice.

The great boulders afforded good protection, and the elephant himself seemed harmless enough. I crept closer to get a better view.

When I saw him next he was standing perfectly still with his ears fixed flat back against his head and cheek. On his cheeks there were two small oily patches: his musth-glands. But there was no discharge down the folds of his cheeks and into his mouth, as I had seen in tethered elephants when on full or mature musth. I watched him for a long time, during which he remained looking at the boulder as if in a dream. He was, I am convinced, imagining that the boulder was a beautiful female elephant and how he would make court to her. The sexual manifestations of it were plain to see.

I left him at last and went back to Kya Sine and told him in a whisper what I had seen, imitating the motions of Bandoola's body with mine. "Hmone Aung Byee," said Kya Sine, excited. "Musth has passed." Readjusting his short lungyi shirt in the Kadaung Kyaik position, which is in itself the expression used to describe the male elephant's anatomy from beneath his tail to under his belly, he now told me to sit and wait while he went to see for himself.

The time passed slowly and my thoughts went back to the boulders I had known as a boy at the cliff base of a Cornish cove near my home. It was not only an elephant who could dream of rocks, and my heart ached with longing for home and for someone who could share my loneliness.

Then suddenly I heard Kya Sine give the order "Hmah," meaning "Lift it up," and immediately after a crash like a rifle-shot, as a branch of a tree which barred the elephant's path along the bank was snapped. I jumped to my feet, ready at a moment to climb the boulder for protection. But as soon as I saw Bandoola's head, with Kya Sine riding him, I knew that the time of danger had passed. I did not say a word, but followed them back to the camp, where all the other elephants were chained to trees as a precaution against the docile demon Bandoola.

We chained him to a tree and to my surprise Po Toke arrived soon after. He had heard the same exaggerated rumours that I had about Bandoola at large on musth.

We discussed Bandoola at length. We could not leave him with his present oozie, who was an utter failure. Though Bandoola was placid enough now, the next time he went on musth it was pretty certain that he would kill some other animal. So we decided to attach Bandoola to my pack-elephants, and with Po Toke riding him to march to the training camp. There we would take the precaution of sawing off the tips of Bandoola's tusks.

We left the following day, and on the march early one evening Po Toke came to me and said, "Go upstream along the bank alone. Don't take even Kya Sine." I didn't question him. I knew from his voice that he was letting me into some secret of the jungle. I went upstream until I came upon Bandoola. This time he was not contemplating a boulder. He had with him a wild kheddar-captured elephant purchased in the Shan States which we were taking to Po Toke's camp for branding. I watched them mating that evening until it was almost dark, and for the ten successive evenings.

Bandoola, I thought almost with envy, had lost his

loneliness and found a mate; and I wondered whether Chit Ma would bear a calf the equal of the sire, though she was not the dam I would have chosen.

Po Toke did not take the possibility seriously. "They are both too young," he said. "But when Bandoola musths, it would be as well to keep him in the company of good dams of middle age."

CHAPTER SIX

THE TAMARIND AND THE TUSKER

THE site of Po Toke's camp was a deserted village, centuries old. The only signs that the place had ever been inhabited were a huge cultivated tamarind tree, and nearby it a small pagoda so dilapidated that it was now little more than a mound of mud-bricks overgrown with creeper.

To watch the operation of sawing off the tips of Bandoola's tusks, I took up my position on the top of the pagoda mound. Bandoola was securely chained to the tamarind tree without a spark of protest. All visible signs of musth had passed and once again he was as docile as any domesticated animal.

The tamarind tree was excellent for the purpose. Its bole, though short, was of great girth, and its massive branches, radiating out in the form of an umbrella, afforded complete shade. It looked as if it had taken

95

about a century to grow and was good for at least another century.

A rope was fastened to Bandoola's left tusk at the lip. It was crossed over in front of the trunk to the right tusk and back again and then made fast. This was to prevent the small handsaw from cutting the trunk, if Bandoola in a fit of irritation tried to swing his trunk forward. Not that it appeared likely to me, watching from the top of the ruined pagoda, that the elephant would create any disturbance. He made no fuss about the rope being tied round his tusks, and as the first three inches of the tusks, which were to be sawed off, contained no nerve, the operation should cause him no pain.

Po Toke dipped his finger in red betel nut and lime and marked off where he was going to cut each tusk. Then he took up the handsaw. Bandoola watched him, squinting down his tusks. It was rather like a child at the dentist's for the first time, I thought, watching him take the drill. Po Toke caught hold of the tusk with his left hand and began to saw with his right.

For a moment Bandoola was quiet, then suddenly he jerked up his head. Po Toke stepped back, losing grip of tusk and saw at the same moment. Bandoola shook his head and let out bellow after bellow of rage. Po Toke shouted to him to be still, but the elephant took no notice. The other attendants stood back, well out of the way. This wasn't going to be a simple operation. I could feel the air charged with danger.

Bandoola was securely chained to the tree. In the battle of their wills, Po Toke had the advantage, just as he had had the advantage over the calf Bandoola in the pen when he was trained. It was just a matter of time. Po Toke waited for Bandoola to quieten down. He left the saw where it had fallen and spoke to the elephant reassuringly. Bandoola was as silent as a coiled spring.

After a time Po Toke stooped down and picked up the saw. For a moment he held the tusk in his left hand. Then suddenly the spring of Bandoola's anger was uncoiled. He lunged. He strained. He put every ounce of his tremendous body-weight against his chains. But they held. Po Toke, faced with this sudden outburst, stepped back. Into his orders he put his full authority. But Bandoola took no notice. He turned around to face the tamarind tree, seized the tying-chains in his trunk and jerked to snap them, but still they held. Then he raised a forefoot and stamped on the chains already strained to breaking point. The fore-fetters snapped. His forelegs were free.

The oozies fled. Po Toke ran up and joined me on the pagoda. We were helpless. There was nothing to do but watch the furious animal break loose. He wasn't apparently angry with those who had tied him up. His rage was concentrated on the tree and the chains which held him. His mind was made up that something must go.

Having got his forefeet free, he ignored the chains

and, raising his tusks high up the tree-trunk to give him leverage, he pushed not only with his whole weight but also with every muscle in his powerful body. A shower of leaves fluttered to the ground; ripe tamarind fruit-pods rained upon the earth and bounced off his body. The whole tree rocked.

The trunk of the tamarind tree came back against Bandoola's trunk and for a moment he rested. Then he heaved against it again. Something snapped, a large root passing underneath him. He rocked the tree rhythmically; there was another snap, a third. His rage became a sort of furious demonstration of power. I watched appalled and yet filled with awe.

Then suddenly there was a rending, and the heaviest branch of the tree snapped and began to fall towards Bandoola. He saw it coming and screamed. He tugged to avoid it. His chains took the extreme strain, but the links did not part. With a volley of explosions as the roots snapped, the whole tree keeled over. Bandoola's screams changed from anger to terror and then they stopped as the tree fell on top of him and buried him from sight.

There is a silence of the forests which follows the crashing of a giant tree, a grave and tragic silence, as if something has suddenly died. Judging from the quiet and the absence of movement, I thought Bandoola was dead too, crushed beneath a tree far more massive even than himself. It was a very peculiar feeling to come down to this battlefield where the corpse of a mighty tree lay obliterating the animal who had killed it.

If Bandoola's chains had broken, he would no doubt have freed himself from the heavy branches which trapped him. But when we examined him, we found that he was lying flat on his side, still chained to the tree by his hind legs.

With incredible speed the elephant men got to work with saws and axes. We had no idea how badly Bandoola was injured. He lay quite motionless during the rescue. The final thing was to smash his chain, and I began to feel that it would never give. But at last with a felling wedge we split a link by driving it into the tree-trunk. Then he slowly rose as if he was recovering from a severe winding. He was as docile as the day he was born. He gave no trouble at all. But no one ever suggested again that his tusks should be tipped.

It was just as well, as it proved; for within two years he had a battle with a wild tusker which might have ended very differently if Po Toke's operation under the tamarind tree had been successful.

Bandoola was not on musth at the time. A wild elephant found him grazing peacefully alone and challenged. There followed a duel, which no one witnessed, but the violence of which I could read easily enough from the wounds of Bandoola and the tracks of the wild tusker.

I went after the wild tusker myself. I trekked him for two days as far as the mouth of the Sihaung river. There he disappeared into a sea of elephant grass about a couple of square miles in area, into which it would have been suicidal to follow him.

From his tracks I could see that the wild tusker had received the *coup de grâce* from Bandoola's sharp-pointed tusks, as his droppings were heavy with blood. There were pools of coagulated blood wherever the poor creature had halted. His head-wounds must have been gruesome; all the way along his tracks there was blood on everything which had brushed against his head. I am sure that he must have died, but though my elephant men hunted for several seasons, they never found his carcase.

Bandoola's wounds were terrible, long deep incisions on the head and withers, alarming to look at but on examination superficial. The really dangerous wound was the one which was least noticeable. It was behind the shoulder-blade on the near side. The wild tusker had obviously made a flank attack, penetrating deeply with the left tusk, which would have pierced the heart and lungs, if the right tusk had not struck the shoulder-blade itself.

I treated Bandoola for a year in Po Toke's training camp, which had now become a hospital for the sick as well as a school for the young. I had learned a great deal from Po Toke about training elephants; but I found it

terribly difficult to teach him and other Burmese elephant men about curing them. Po Toke as a Buddhist
believed that sick and injured elephants could be cured
by faith; and even though I proved time and again that
my methods worked where his failed, I could not help
feeling at times that he resented what I tried to do.

Bandoola's wounds healed remarkably well with
treatment. But his whole blood-system became affected.
He developed abscess after abscess, sinuses and fistulas.
This was partly due to the fact that he got out of condition. But I think there was also something which
would be understandable to everyone in the case of an
injured human being and which to me is quite understandable in the case of Bandoola. Up to the time of the
fight with the wild tusker, Bandoola had been a perfect
physical specimen, without a blemish and without a scar.
He had the sort of pride which some men and women have
in their physical perfection; and the sight of his wounds
filled him with shame. He had lost faith in himself. Yet he
was the most wonderful patient I have ever handled,
man, woman or animal. And the day came at last when
I felt that I had won. Bandoola had regained his health,
his strength and his pride. I gave orders for him to
return to forest work, discharged from hospital.

That evening I was sitting at my camp-table in front
of my tent, feeling pleased with myself and the world in
general. There had been times when I had lost hope of
ever getting Bandoola better. "Well," I told myself,

"you've thoroughly deserved the fishing holiday at Patala which you're going to take to-morrow."

Then I looked up and saw Po Toke coming towards the tent. That was not strange. It was something he often did. But never before had he come as now in company with Ma Pyoo. That was not merely unusual: it was ominous.

They both squatted near the table and I asked Ma Pyoo how she and her relations were. She answered politely that all was well, when suddenly Po Toke broke in. "Thakin, I wish to resign and give up my work."

I couldn't believe my ears. Po Toke was my master in the study of elephants, my most trusted assistant in their management. "What did you say?"

He repeated his resignation, a resignation which meant abandoning Bandoola. I couldn't imagine why he was going, but I suddenly realised that the reason why he felt he could leave Bandoola was because I was there to look after the elephant for him. "If you go, Po Toke," I said, "I shall go too." I almost meant it.

Both of them tried to smile off my threat of resignation, but I repeated it seriously.

Then Po Toke thought of a way out. Instead of resigning, would I allow him to go on long leave?

"That is a different matter," I answered. "And while you're away," I added, to put the conversation on a lighter plane, "while you're away, wouldn't it be a good idea to leave Ma Pyoo with me, just to make sure you come back?"

They laughed, and then Ma Pyoo said that she had heard I was going to Patala for the fishing. "Don't worry," she said; "you will catch a fish there and then you won't be lonely."

"What makes you say that?"

She smiled and answered, "That fish has no scales."

It was a remark I remember partly because there lay beneath her joke, and I suppose mine as well, a recognition of my loneliness and longing for a mate; but also because of something which happened when I reached Patala.

Patala was a very isolated village of intermarried Chins and Burmans. I camped about a quarter of a mile away, and on the first evening the headman invited me to come to their rice festival.

It was the biggest drunk I have ever attended. I joined in the party, danced round their zoo pots of country rice-liquor and took my drink through the same straws as they used out of an enormous communal pot the size of a cauldron. To me, accustomed to whisky, the drink was as soft as lime-juice, though not as pleasant. But the Patalans grew drunker and drunker, the women even worse than the men. Even women with babies strapped to their shoulder-blades drank and danced themselves into a state of hysteria. I saw several of them suckling their babies as they danced. I felt disgusted, and yet in a curious way I enjoyed it. It gave me some outlet for my desperation, my sense that I was just wasting my life on elephants and teak, leeches and malaria.

I learnt their songs. There is one I can sing to this day. "Choyin! Choyin! Chalin Mayin!" I don't understand a word of what it means and yet the air conveys to me a lovely sense of the forests and the hills.

When I tried to leave and went to bid the headman good night, he begged me through an interpreter to stay as a compliment to them. So I remained until the communal pot was dry and the last dancers staggered off. Then the headman invited me to his house.

We went up some bamboo steps on to a veranda. My nostrils were assailed by a stench the origin of which puzzled me until I heard the grunting of pigs beneath us. I began to feel that the evening was going to end in anticlimax. But the interpreter announced that the headman wanted to tell my fortune, which he was certain was good.

After a little while a sorcerer arrived with a dozen chickens in a basket. He throttled six birds and counted their struggles as they died. The spectacle revolted me, but they cheered and patted me on the back. This made me so angry that I told the interpreter that if they killed another bird, I should go.

He looked surprised and then explained to the headman that I was in earnest. Apparently the massacre had been sufficient, because the sorcerer put the others away in his basket and suddenly a most beautiful girl was produced from behind an inner bamboo matting partition.

In height she was almost six feet and as fair of skin as a fair Spaniard. She wore her jet-black hair in two long pigtails which hung down her back far below her waist. She was of no nationality known to me, but she spoke the language of these people of Patala.

Standing on that veranda with the pigs grunting below us and their stench rising steadily, she was an astonishing spectacle. She looked as if she had been taken from some prison den and dressed for the occasion in beautiful clothes. There was no smile on her face. Indeed, she scowled. I could see from the way she looked at the headman, the interpreter and the others, that she hated them. Yet in the way she held herself, with her head up, exposing her long, slender neck, there was magnificent pride.

When I looked away from her, I noticed that everyone had left us except the interpreter. "Who is this girl?" I asked. She had sat down. There were four smoky open-wick lamps burning on the veranda and their light seemed to caress her. I didn't like what was happening. It smacked too much of the slave-market.

"What she is called we do not know," said the interpreter. "Her mother was a Chin woman from this village, but she is dead. Her father was a European officer—a Sit Bo—who passed this way to the Kuki rebellion many, many years ago. He is dead also. He was killed after sleeping in this village."

I could see the whole picture, that young British officer a quarter of a century before, as lonely as I was and frightened into the bargain, because he was going to quell a rebellion. Perhaps he got drunk or maybe it was the instinct a man has, when he feels death close, to reproduce his species. I could understand that; and now I could understand this beautiful girl, *her* loneliness, her hatred and her pride. There she was in this village, the living reminder of an act which even when it had happened must have meant very little.

"She is unhappy," said the interpreter. "Your fortune to-night says that you will take her away and make her happy."

I shook my head. His arithmetic was wrong. If you add one loneliness to another, you don't necessarily get love or even companionship.

"Take her for ten days, then," said the interpreter; "you can leave her here again when you go."

The girl was lovely and I told the man to tell her so. She wore across her shoulder a brilliant red Chin blanket like a chieftain. The interpreter spoke to her and took the blanket from her bare shoulders to pass it to me; but she snatched it and flung it back across her shoulder. She got up and stood, looking like an angry matador. Then she turned and ran into the darkness of the veranda. She understood something the interpreter didn't.

Two of my servants who had come to the village with me lighted me back to camp. Their account of this girl was as fragmentary as that of the village interpreter. She was definitely an Anglo-Chin. Her mother, a drunken Chin girl, had given her blanket to a Sit Bo when he was sleeping in the village, the recognised sign of sharing the cold night. The girl was now a servant slave to the headman, but she was proud. She never mixed with the girls of the village and would have nothing to do with the men.

I moved camp next day to fish and forget about red blankets. In my new camp I caught a baby otter. She was a darling, one of the most lovable pets I ever possessed. I kept her for six months and lost her without grief. She used to fish with me in the Upper Taungdwin. One afternoon while I was swimming I let her loose in a pool which was as clear as gin. She came back to the rocks three or four times and chatter-barked to me. Then I caught sight of three other otters schooling in the pool. The three soon became four, because Taupai joined their game and company. It was the last I saw of her, sporting with them in the clear water. I said good-bye with a contented heart. She had found her happiness.

I had not. A tremendous restlessness had come over me. That was why I became excited when two Chins brought to my camp two stones, which to anyone without a knowledge of mineralogy would have appeared to be jadestones. My servants had told them I was for ever picking up stones, hunting for something—though as far as they knew I had never found anything but black "mahooyah" onyx. Perhaps I might pay money for these stones.

I didn't buy the stones, but I paid the Chins a hire to show me where they had found them. A forest fire in dense kaing grass had exposed a white outcrop of limestone. The heat had splintered it and the men had found a few stones with streaks of vivid green. I found one myself. I stood it in a bowl of water overnight, and by the morning it had taken on, as I expected, a green colour throughout. It was green opal.

I got my elephant men to work and we blasted several shot of dynamite deep into the limestone by mud-plaster contact-shots. With each blast we exposed more and more beautiful opalescent fragments. I forgot about fishing and in three days I had located and exposed a clean seam or small lode in a vertical stratum between two walls of hard limestone.

When my leave was ended and I returned to my normal work, I took with me an Army kit-bag full of specimens, an elephant load. Before I left I wrote a promise to give the two Chins ten per cent of any profits I made, if I ever came back to work the seam, and I had the headman witness it. No simpler or more amateur staking of a claim was ever made. I even sent a messenger on a fifteen-day journey with a formal letter requesting a mining licence of the area. The Government official who received it, a friend of mine, just answered, "Apply when you find the diamonds. But go on digging!"

To him it was a joke, but I was deadly serious. I came back and set twenty jungle Chin villagers to work as quarrymen and miners. I sent a specimen to a professor at the Royal School of Mines, a friend of my father's. I even was fool enough to mention it in the monthly diary which went to my employers. I couldn't think of anything else. At night alone in the camp I sat turning and twisting choice specimens between my fingers under the lamplight. I began to build castles in the air with the fortune I dreamed of making. I should breed elephants, an enormous stud of them; and also timber-dragging water-buffaloes, an even more enormous stud, because they were easier and didn't take so long.

And then I got a letter from the "Ek dum Burra Sahib" the "gawd damn number one of everything"; it reminded me that I was paid as a full-time servant, employed in the extraction of teak. If I wished to turn my attention towards mining, I should do so at once and tender my resignation. Even if the project were feasible, it would only divert forest labour, already scarce, away from the teak industry, which, if not my primary concern, was that of other company employees. A copy had gone to my immediate senior in the Forest.

I read the letter several times and I wrote several pungent replies which I was tempted to dispatch at once. But I tore them up one after the other. I was alone. I was young and fit. I was on musth. I was fed up with the jungle. And yet green opals would bring me back to the jungle. The idea of making a fortune excited me, but where on earth was I to find the capital with which to start operations?

At last I decided to spin a coin. "Heads it's opals. Tails it's elephants." It came down elephants, and elephants it stayed. Good-bye to opals and fishes without scales.

CHAPTER SEVEN

LOST

EVEN though I had learnt Burmese and took some trouble to understand the men who worked for me, I knew that I only understood a small fraction of what was going on in their minds. Though we worked together, I was British, they were Burman. I, though the employee of a private company, was the Government, they were the governed. It was a thing that had not worried me much until that evening when Po Toke came with Ma Pyoo and tendered his resignation. It gave me a shock. It made me realise that just as the camp was a clearing in the jungle, so my own tent was a little clearing in the camp.

I had noticed strangers in camps which I had visited; but there are always strangers—travellers, opium-peddlers and so on. I suspected sometimes that these visitors had another purpose, that they were out to make trouble. But there was nothing on which I could put my finger, and anyway I argued that, whatever happened, elephant men would not abandon their elephants.

About a month after Po Toke departed on his long leave to stay with his wife's relations, I was transferred to the same area—back to Ningyan. Immediately I got there I realised that rumours of discontent were well founded. I could feel the tension the moment I went into a camp, and my assistants found the same thing wherever they went. I discussed it with government officials, but the answer was that the resentment was directed not against the Government but against the large teak-trading companies.

Perhaps the Government was right, I thought. Perhaps the hostile feeling which greeted me in camps was not because I was British but because I was working for the T"Tai Bombine. All I knew for certain was that the feeling was hostile, and I didn't like it. I felt depressed and worried.

The first news which I received from my old forest depressed me even further. Bandoola was lost. Po Toke had heard rumours of his escape and though he was on leave he came to me to find out how true they were. I could tell him only what I had heard, but I added as a joke that maybe Bandoola had made up his mind to join us in Ningyan.

Po Toke did not smile. "He was born in Ningyan,"

he said, "born and trained at the mouth of the Palway Creek, thirty-seven years ago. And if he's found, it will be at the Palway Creek."

One day, I thought to myself, when I am free, I'll go to the Palway Creek and look. But that day did not come for nearly a year, and if it had not been for a dog, Ba Sein, it would never have come at all.

Ba Sein was a Bassein Fishery Hound, a breed once listed by the Indian Kennel Association. They are supposed to have originated from a cross between bloodhounds, imported into the Burmese port of Bassein by Portuguese traders, and the common Indian pariah.

They bred very true to type. From the bloodhound strain they got their deep chocolate colour, the heavy jowl and lop-hanging ears; from the pariah, small, neat, sure-footed paws. The tail was peculiar, because it had the twist or twirl of a chow, though entirely unfeathered.

Bassein fishery men used them to guard their boats, tackle or catches. They were savage with strangers and they could be left for days and nights alone on the sandbank of the delta without deserting their charges. They were striking to look at and good specimens were very rare, because it was hard to tell from a puppy how one would turn out.

I came by Ba Sein because he was in disgrace, in fact under sentence of death. He had dangerously

savaged an Indian postman. His owner, a British rice-
trader in Bassein, forged a certificate that he had been
destroyed, and gave him to an up-country forest man.
I met him a week later. The forest man offered him to
me, explaining that he had had to chain the dog up,
because at the hint of correction the dog flew at his
Adam's apple.

I was taken in to see him at night, securely chained in
a stable. He was marvellous. He bayed at me with the
voice of a hound. He twisted his tail almost out of joint,
begging for another home and yet another chance.

I walked straight in to him, patted him, unchained
him and led him home to my bungalow. Next day I
left on a forest tour with everyone, including my
servants, who were convinced I was mad to take on a
dog like that.

But I had a number of reasons for needing a dog who
could act as a sort of police-guard. The drainage to
which I was going was the Nanpo, which hadn't been
worked for timber for thirty years. It was notorious as
a hide-out for dacoits. I was taking a lot of money with
me, for I had an appointment with an elephant contractor to whom I had promised an advance of five
hundred rupees for each of the twenty elephants he was
providing. The Nanpo was ten days' march away and I
should have to camp each night in an isolated jungle.
Even in the most peaceful of times that would have been
hazardous, considering the amount of money I should

have with me. But in addition to that, I had received a few days before an anonymous letter in Burmese threatening me with violence if I tried to open up the Nanpo drainage. As I see now, the Nanpo was intended as one of the mustering-centres for the rebellion.

Ba Sein had another name when I took him, but he took to his new name quite uncannily, considering that he was a full-grown animal. For the first day's march, I talked to him the whole time, always by name and in Burmese.

That night there was no danger. I camped in a forest bungalow on the fringe of a village and slept in a securely-closed room. Ba Sein was deliriously happy to be off his chain and given good food and constant attention. By evening I had only to call his new name and his kinked tail would twist with joy at being spoken to. He was an extraordinary dog. He never slept or fully rested. Every time I looked up from my reading or writing, there he was, with his ears half-cocked, perpetually in that attitude of alertness which I had only seen in a dog before when there was a tiger or a leopard about.

Before I went to bed, I gave Ba Sein a mat in the centre of the room and told him to lie down. Several times during the night I woke up and flashed my torch on him; each time he was in exactly the same position, motionless but intent and wide awake.

For the following ten nights I camped in a tent. Ba Sein became more and more of a companion. His eyes fascinated me: as warm and brown as his short coat, they seemed fixed on something deeper and beyond anything I could see. It never occurred to me that he might turn on me as he had on those who chained him. I took off his collar as soon as we got into the jungle. A collar gets entangled in undergrowth and will throttle a dog. I could see that he had returned to the life in which he had been brought up, the life of a fisherman's guard-dog without collar or chain. The only thing that worried me was that he never slept. Whatever hour I put my torch on him he was awake and alert.

When I reached my destination, an eerie watershed with precipitous slopes to the headwater, there was no sign of the contractor or his elephants. But this did not worry me. They had a two months' march from the east and might well have been delayed a day or two. So I settled down to wait a few days.

The Nanpo creek was a fast mountain-stream and very rocky, with huge black boulders, fast runs of rapids and large pools where mahseer were plentiful. On the evening of my arrival I fished from near camp and caught two splendid eight-pounders.

The next day I decided to trek up-river. I would not take Ba Sein because the going was slippery and treacherous for a dog; but he insisted on following me. Three or four times I ordered him back to my tent sharply in Burmese, but I had not gone a quarter of a mile before he was with me again.

I knew it would be courting trouble to collar him and chain him up. So I asked the cook for one of the mahseer I had caught the previous evening and threw it on the floor at the entrance to my hut. "All right," I said. "Guard that, and if you're hungry, eat it." He sat on his haunches beside it and made no attempt to follow me.

I shot a barking deer for the pot that day and it was late evening before we got back, my gun-boy struggling with it across his shoulders. There was commotion in the camp. "Your dog is rabid mad," my servants shouted. Ba Sein had howled all day and threatened to savage anyone who came in sight of the tent. "Load your gun," they said, "you'll have to shoot him."

As I approached the tent, I called out, "Ba Sein, Ba Sein." But he did not answer. Then I caught sight of him. There he was sitting on guard beside the fish, just as I'd left him. He wagged his twisted tail at me. "Are you mad, Ba Sein?" I asked. "Mad?" he seemed to answer, "yes, mad with delight!" and he rushed round my legs. We loved each other dearly.

That night for his supper he had the baked mahseer, bones and all, in a bowl of rice. But he didn't sleep.

The anonymous letter which had worried me before I set out passed out of my thoughts. It was good camping in the jungle with the sound of the babbling stream, and fish and game to fill the pot. Saw Maung, the contractor, arrived with eighteen elephants and six baby calves at heel. For the calves he had the impudence, with a twinkle in his eye, to claim half-advances. The contracts were signed; everything had gone according to plan; and we started back.

The trek was uneventful until we reached the bungalow, the last rest before the march to the main river. Ba Sein shared tea with me on the veranda and then we went for a stroll round the compound. I noticed that the village seemed strangely quiet. It was practically deserted. I saw a man walking along the dusty road and called to him, but he hurried on.

I went back to the veranda and suddenly I noticed that Ba Sein was not at heel. The same moment there came a cry: "Thakin! Thakin!" It was one of the servants. I ran out, and there kicking and frothing on the ground was Ba Sein, apparently in a fit. I bent over him, and as I did so he went stiff. He was dead.

As I picked him up and carried him to the veranda, the recollection of the anonymous letter came back to me. They had poisoned Ba Sein because they knew that while he was alive they could not get at me. I yelled for my head elephant man. "Catch all elephants," I shouted. "We are moving on the main river to-night."

My camp was never broken quicker. The elephants were loaded, the last one carrying the cold body of Ba Sein wrapped in a blanket. As we moved off, there were no villagers lined up to watch our departure, no headman came to pay respects. The village was deserted.

And so it was all the way to the main river. We saw

no one. My followers seemed to realise for the first time in their lives that time was pressing. Jungle rumours move fast.

It was almost midnight when we arrived at the township headquarters on the main river. But the district bungalow was ablaze with light. The place was occupied by a posse of Civil Police. As I went in, I met a police officer I knew. He wrung me by the hand. "Thank God you're here!" he said. "The whole damned countryside's in the hands of rebels." He mentioned the name of a forest man I knew. "They got him this morning," he said, "murdered him for the firearms."

And that, I realised, is what would have happened to me if it hadn't been for Ba Sein.

For months after that, contact with elephant camps was practically severed. I was right in thinking that the elephant men would not desert their animals. But it became too dangerous for individual European timber assistants to travel through the jungle.

When at last we had succeeded in re-establishing contact by touring in armed parties, I found that in one case the rebels had borrowed a hundred baskets of rice and twenty elephants, leaving a message to say that they would be paid for as soon as the Government was overthrown. My own elephant men had carried out the transport for them at the point of stolen firearms rather than desert their animals.

These tours in armed strength made me long for the peaceful days of solitary jungle life. Almost worse than the continual menace of attack from the rebels was the enforced companionship of a temporarily appointed government official and one's fellow Forest Assistants.

I remember one night in particular. We had a body of irregular Karen levies who were picketed around the camp and in a tent, ten feet square, four of us were trying to play bridge, three forest assistants and a young temporary official who would have been scared to death in the jungle without any rebels around. He was so jumpy that when an owl hooted, he thought it was an armed attack. His bridge, perhaps, had never been in the first class; but that evening it was appalling. We tried to carry off his revokes with excuses like "That was when the owl hooted." But he didn't find them funny. His temper became shorter and shorter, and at midnight we all threw in our hands and turned in, without even a word of good night.

Lying there in the darkness, I could tell by the others' breathing that they were not asleep. We were all wide awake, loathing each other's guts and at the same time listening for any suspicious sound which might mean an attack. To be attacked, I thought, would be a relief, because it would break the tension and make some sense out of our being cooped up together.

At last I said, "This is the sort of bloody silly row that starts rebellions, not cures them. I'm pretty sure that we're going to be attacked before dawn. Let's get up and go on playing till the trouble starts."

We got up and played all night without quarrels or post-mortems. There wasn't any raid of course, but the sense that there might be had brought us together again.

On another of these tours a strange thing happened. We had twenty pack-elephants, and I took the precaution of tying them up to form an outer defence-perimeter to warn the pickets in event of attack.

At dawn the next day my head elephant man reported that a wild elephant had been heard visiting our tethered animals during the night. The same thing happened the next night, though we had marched ten miles during the day. A strong band of dacoits had recently camped nearby, so we lay up for a day. My suspicions were that they were using the elephant as a scout. We were armed for defence, but not to look for trouble, and I thought there was less likelihood of our being raided where we were than if we moved on.

That night the elephant came again, and as he moved round the perimeter we could hear the tethered elephants ringing warning sounds with their trunks upon the earth. But no attack developed. We moved on again and the elephant moved with us, visiting each animal in turn during the night and disappearing before dawn.

We played with the idea of a ghost elephant one

evening; but the ghost left solid enough tracks. If it had not been for the rebels, I would have gone after him to satisfy my curiosity; but it was too dangerous.

One day, when we were nearing our destination, which was the mouth of the Palway Creek, the column suddenly came to a halt. I was in the middle and I pushed ahead to see what was wrong. From the lead I soon heard shouts of "Taw Sin! Taw Sin!" (Wild elephant!)

When I reached the leading section of armed Karens, the head Burman ran to me and said that just ahead a magnificent wild tusker was standing quite still on the track. What should we do? To shoot him would cause panic in those behind, because they would imagine we were being attacked.

I went forward cautiously with the head man, and there, a hundred yards away, I saw a magnificent tusker indeed. But he was one I recognised immediately, though I had last seen him five hundred miles away. "Bandoola," I said in a loud voice; and seeing me, he trumpeted and fled, exposing as he did so the bold "C" on his near side rump. Po Toke had been right. Bandoola had returned to his birthplace.

Several times during the day we saw him. There was no chance of going after him. We had to tether our own elephants and hand-feed them, because of the danger of men getting separated and captured as hostages. At first we set ourselves to watch Bandoola when he approached, in order to assess what his temper was after a year of freedom.

Po Toke was the man to capture Bandoola. But Po Toke had overstayed his leave and my suspicion was that he was in some way concerned with the rebels. For any other oozie to try to mount Bandoola himself would have been suicidal. He had become shy of men, we decided by that evening, but he seemed docile enough apart from that.

No one would volunteer to capture Bandoola, but a young Karen oozie suggested that we should try the method of capture which is known as mela shikar, and volunteered if that succeeded to ride Bandoola.

For mela shikar, the Karens select two full-grown female elephants of a steady temperament; on each are mounted two riders, one on the head in the normal position, the second on the centre of the back, holding a surcingle of rope tied fast round the elephant's body. Even young wild elephants are often captured in this way, because a wild elephant usually does not notice a man mounted on another elephant, since he is above the scent-line.

I agreed to try mela shikar, despite the dangers of leaving camp; and as we got down to it, the thought of rebels and rebellions passed out of my mind and for a few hours I was really happy again, back in an old routine.

It was early evening when the two female elephants

entered the sea of kaing grass eight to twelve feet high in which Bandoola was grazing. I climbed up a tree from which I could see the whole manœuvre. Bandoola was out of sight but the tops of the kaing grass swayed when he moved. The two females I could follow because the oozies on their backs were visible above the grass. They signalled to one another, while the riders on the heads casually and with amazing patience steered them to converge on Bandoola from either flank. It was so skilfully done that the females, who were grazing freely all the time, were unaware of what was happening.

Such an operation at any time is fraught with suspense; in this case there was added the hazard that at any moment there might be a rebel attack. It was all done in complete silence and in slow motion. It was rather like watching from a cliff the movement of yachts in the distance. They drew closer and closer. Then suddenly, when they were within a stone's throw of one another, the silence was broken by a chirp, a chirp I somehow associated with this lovable great animal Bandoola. It is made by placing the tongue between the teeth against the side of the cheek and then sucking air in, rather like the gee-up sound for a horse. The noise will carry a mile and is a signal of contentment and joy.

As soon as I heard it, I knew there would be no trouble. It was as if Bandoola was calling to the females, "Come here. There's a luscious patch of green kaing where I am." Elephant courtship is tactful, slow and certain. One of the females chirped back. Then guttural rumblings came from Bandoola like the noise of a Rolls-Bentley.

The heads of the four oozies were now very close together. So for a moment they remained. It was all over except to see them march out of the kaing grass in single file to the river-bed below me. First came Shan Ma with one rider only, then Bandoola, whose rider had merely stepped off Shan Ma's back on to his new mount, and finally Yinzin Ma with her two riders.

It had been beautifully done. But then, I thought to myself, the oozies were children of the forest, as much at home in it as Bandoola himself. They were part of nature, and the bond of friendship with animals had not been broken by civilisation.

When I congratulated the young Karen on his good work, he said, "My people say no captive elephant wishes to return to the wild, but if an elephant tries, it takes another elephant to convince him that he is wrong."

It was the same with the Burmese rebels. Police and soldiers only strengthened their determination. The rebellion was broken by the persuasion of sensible Burmans.

Bandoola was attached to my armed party for the remainder of our tour. He was in his prime. His size and strength set him apart among the pack-elephants, like a shire horse in a cavalry troop. Even if I had had pack-saddlery for him, it would have wounded my sense of the fitting as much as his to see him in any harness other than traces and dragging-gear.

His very name and presence gave protection to our column. For no Burman without a lifetime's experience of elephants would have dared, whatever his political opinion, to tackle so ferocious-looking a tusker, docile and friendly though he was in fact.

With the breaking of the monsoon and the capture of the rebel leader Saya San, organised rebellion collapsed. Resistance continued in isolated pockets, but the country returned to normal.

I tried to make contact with Po Toke. But he was living in a remote village where the rebels had been very active. He was under suspicion and forbidden to leave. So were a number of people as innocent as Po Toke pretended to be when at last he did come back. I found it impossible to believe his story. Why had he come to me just before the outbreak of the rebellion? Why didn't he return at the end of his long leave? There was nothing to prevent a man like him from going back to his post.

I was deeply disappointed in him—though perhaps it was my fault for taking him to be a simpler character than he was. I liked to think of him as a man who loved elephants, and Bandoola especially. He tried to claim full credit for the recapture of Bandoola, because he had foretold that he would return to his birthplace. He as good as stated that I had gone to the Palway Creek with an armed column to pick Bandoola up on his information. The trust which had once existed between us was shaken. I found myself suspecting that the reason why Po Toke had been so sure that Bandoola would be at the Palway Creek was because he had employed an oozie to march the elephant there secretly. He even discussed the route by which he reckoned Bandoola must have travelled in stages.

"Well," I asked, "how and where did he cross the Irrawaddy River?"

"Bandoola could do anything," he answered.

At first I told him that as he had not returned from his long leave at the proper time, he had broken his service as far as I was concerned. I could not reinstate him, certainly not as a trainer. I confess I was shocked by his appearance. He was only about fifty, which is not old for a jungle Burman, but in the past twelve months he had aged tremendously. The sense of authority which he had commanded had declined. And yet I couldn't deny that Bandoola could not be in better hands than Po Toke's, even though Po Toke had been the only elephant man I knew who had deserted during the rebellion.

At first I thought of employing him in the Ningyan forest and placing Bandoola in his charge. But it was too near his wife's relatives, to put it in the kindest way.

So I decided to transfer them back to the Chindwin Forests.

He left me with a complete camp of ten elephants including Bandoola. They were taken on a large flat and towed by a launch, a form of elephant transport common enough by the thirties, very different from the methods used when Bandoola made the journey first as a trained calf.

As a result of the information which I sent ahead of him, Po Toke was taken on, not as a Singaung in charge of a timber extraction camp, but in a more subordinate position. But Bandoola was his leader animal and that made up for his loss of responsibility.

He could also pride himself on extracting some of the largest timber ever handled by elephants in Burma. The demand for long teak-logs suitable for squaring had become so intense that a solid teak-log of over fifty feet was like nugget-gold beside gold-ore. Elephants like Bandoola capable of handling these enormous logs were even scarcer than the logs themselves. But thanks to Po Toke's good management he was never sick. In one season he was recorded as having extracted three hundred tons of teak an average distance of two miles from stump to floating-stream.

CHAPTER EIGHT

INTERLUDE WITH A CIRCUS

I DID not realise what a strain the rebellion had been until it was all over. It was not merely the threat of danger and the irritation of having to travel in armed companies. It was the fact that during that time we had been cut off from the outside world, from those casual contacts the value of which one does not appreciate until deprived of them. If it had not been for the end of the rebellion the Indian touring circus would not have aroused as much interest as it did.

They were the first strangers to arrive at my forest headquarters after the troubles, and the proprietor immediately came to my bungalow, not, as I thought, to pay his respects, but, as I soon discovered, to ask me to examine his elephants, two of which were suffering from tummy trouble. In return he offered me as many complimentary tickets as I wanted and expressed the hope that I would bring all the Europeans in the station.

I spent the whole day with the circus and was able to give the sick elephants immediate relief. The company of one's colleagues in a forest station begins to pall after a time. However different they may be in character to begin with, they grow alike as they are assimilated in the job. One longs for people who are different; and different these circus folk certainly were. There was a Russian trapeze act, five men and one girl; a troupe of Filipino acrobats; a Canadian couple, a man and a girl with good horses; some French clowns who were funny on bicycles; some Japanese wrestlers who were fat but not funny at all and a stunningly beautiful Italian wire-rope artiste, whose loneliness I felt it would be ungallant not to console.

When I left them, I promised that I would muster all the Europeans, of whom there were more than usual at the station because of the troubles. I had six young bachelor Forest Assistants, living in the large bachelor chummery, who were quick to make friends with the circus people. One even persuaded the Canadian girl to play afternoon station-polo mounted on one of her skewbalds. She had never played before and I have never had six such funny and dangerous chukkers. She went mad with excitement and so did the pony. After the first chukker I placed her at back, hoping for safety. Uttering a whoopee she would hit out and then follow on as if she were doing a rodeo act. In a *mêlée* someone lost a topee. She came in on it at full gallop, swooped down from the saddle, picked it up and handed it back to the owner.

Half the circus came to watch, including the lovely Italian tight-rope walker, dressed in a garden-party frock and out to kill, as much as the Canadian girl, but in a different way.

Anyway she killed me. Before the evening was out I had arranged to give a midnight party for the whole troupe after the last night of the show. But I found I had my rivals among the assistants. Michael, Hamish and Peter all ganged up on me. "Of course, we know you're just giving it for her," they said, "but remember all's fair. . . ."

Most of us had already been to the circus once, but we all turned up for the last night just the same. The tent was packed with Indians and Burmans, the colour of whose clothing was a show in itself. There were fifteen to twenty Europeans. We had all been to convivial parties beforehand and we went on drinking during the performance.

When it was over, it was arranged that those with cars should stay behind and bring the artistes over to my bungalow in relays. The crowd had left after the last turn, the spectacular act of the Russian trapezists. The life-net was still in position, the ring was empty, the artists were in their dressing-rooms changing. They seemed to take an awful long time.

Freddie, getting bored, stepped into the ring and started to act the clown. There was laughter and applause. We were growing tired of waiting. Then Hamish and Peter tripped out, imitating two of the Russian trapezists. One went to each of the enormous tent-poles. They bowed to us and scratched the saw-dust off their feet. They were lit up and they were very funny. They had just caught the rather solemn routine of the Russians and reduced it to a parody. Both were dressed in the same way: white duck trousers, white short-sleeved shirts with black bow ties and shining black pumps. They bowed to each other. "Hopp-la!" Together they started to climb the rope ladders, pre-tending to be clowns, pretending to be tight, missing their footing, clinging on by the hands, but always getting higher. It was a wonderful imitation of a pro-fessional tipsy act. Both of them arrived swaying on the trapeze platforms and as they bowed again to each other, there was a burst of applause from us below.

Without hesitation Hamish took the pole hook, leaned forward and pulled back the trapeze. "Hopp-la!" He pretended to fall, but hung on with one hand, precariously holding his balance.

Peter did the same thing. And then once again they solemnly bowed amid our laughter and applause.

Then, to my horror, Hamish gripped the trapeze bar and swung from the platform into mid-air sixty feet above the life-net, followed immediately after by Peter. They were still clowning, pretending to lose grasp and hanging on by one hand. Down below we stopped laughing. We all knew before they did that they would never be able to get back to those platforms. But we did not dare to shout a warning—it was too late for that.

When they called down to us in the seats we tried to joke back to keep their nerves steady.

It was impossible to tell exactly when they stopped playing the clown and tried seriously to swing themselves back, because their efforts were just as clownish. They were getting tired. Hamish managed to swing one leg over the trapeze bar and take the weight off his arms. But neither he, nor Peter who copied him, were able to get both feet over the bar and take a sitting rest. Once again they reverted to the two-handed grip and tried to swing themselves back to the platforms. But they had not the skill to do it and now they were too weak to get a leg over the trapeze. They just hung helpless, their bodies becoming heavier every second. Hamish released one hand, hanging now by one arm. "Hopp-la!" he shouted, and as he let go he waved to Peter. Whether he bent his knees or not, I don't know; but the net shot him back into the air like a popgun-cork. When he stopped bouncing, he lay absolutely still, a white depression in the rope net; whether dead or unconscious we could not tell, while Peter was still hanging on above.

Peter said nothing, but he began feebly to swing to and fro, a very weak imitation of the Russian who such a little while before had dropped from the trapeze and bounced upright on the rope net until he came to a standstill.

As he reached the end of a backward swing he

bellowed "Hopp-la!" and released his grip. Instead of delicately falling feet forwards, he came down with arms and legs outspread like a flying squirrel, striking the net simultaneously with face, chest, stomach and legs, before he bounced up again and came to rest a dozen feet from Hamish.

Three excited Russians, shouting in their own language, swarmed up the ladders to the net and dragged and passed the limp bodies to the ground. That Hamish and Peter were now sober there was no doubt, but there was some question for a moment whether they were alive. Then they began to groan. No bones were broken. But I had not seen such welts since I was at school. For them the party was over.

"Well," said Michael to me, as we drove to my bungalow, "that's two out of the running for the fair Italian: That just leaves you and me."

But we were mistaken. She arrived at the party, squired by a French clown. "You haven't met my husband, I think," she said. In her arms she was carrying a large parcel, as if it was fragile. "And by the way," she asked, "where can I put this?"

"What is it?" I asked.

She opened her beautiful eyes as if surprised. "It's baby!" she said.

CHAPTER NINE

THE NATS OF THE WABOBIN GORGE

WHILE I was entertaining the Indian circus, Po Toke was marching his elephants to the Chindwin Forest. En route Bandoola was intercepted and directed to a very specialised job, breaking up a terrific blockage of teak-logs in the Wabobin Gorge.

The gorge was regarded by the Burmans as a shrine of the Nats. At its entrance, where the river flowed in between cliffs two hundred feet high, and again at its exit a mile below, stood two small snow-white pagodas. I never discovered who had built them, because they were on precipitous peaks of rock which from the river appeared unscaleable even by mountaineers.

It was said that from the large rock ledge which lay below, women pilgrims who came during the hot season threw their jewels up the cliff-face. Those whose offerings remained at the base of the shrine at the entrance were assured of happy marriage, those at the exit of children. Every gold bangle, necklace or ring which missed went bounding down into the bottomless pool below.

That was the story which I had heard some years before when, exploring the Forest Area, I had made the hazardous journey through the gorge. It was an eerie place which never saw the sun, except for a shaft of light about mid-day, the sort of place round which superstition gathers as inevitably as cobwebs in the dark corners of an unused room.

If we were to exploit the forest above, we had to float our timber through the gorge. It wasn't merely a physical barrier; it was also a superstitious barrier. When I made my survey, no Burman would go with me; I went in the dry season, and I met no obstacles other than boulders as big as houses and dark green pools, every one of which I had to swim because the walls of the gorge were sheer cliffs, covered with lichen and moss and with every sort of fern growing in the crannies.

My report had been that it was impossible to blast away the obstructions. If you blasted one, you would have to blast thousands. The only way was to let the teak logs pound their way through on the raging monsoon torrents and pray to the Nats they didn't come out at the other end like double-ended shaving-brushes.

In the first floating-season the monsoon was sharp and heavy. On the terrific floods the logs went through high over the towering boulders. Very little damage was done and only a few odd logs jammed.

But the next season the monsoon was lighter and more gradual in its coming. The floods carried the logs down and piled three thousand of them in a gigantic stack across the gorge.

THE JAMMED GORGE

It looked as if the only way of clearing them would be by blasting, which even if it did not call down the anger of the Nats, as the Burmans swore it would, would certainly antagonise the Burmans themselves.

The man with the misfortune to be faced by this problem was Gerry Dawson, an ex-naval officer, a very gallant and generous fellow. He was well aware of the superstition against blasting, and before he blasted he wanted to see whether he couldn't unlock the jam by using elephants. He reported that he had found a possible track in for elephants, provided the work was done in the hot, dry season.

I was asked to advise on the practicability of using elephants. I went along to see for myself. It was a fantastic sight. There were thousands of logs, anything from fifteen to forty-five feet in length and from four and-a-half feet to twelve or fourteen feet in girth. Some weighed between five and six tons. From above they looked like matchsticks; as if a whole warehouse full of matches had been blown up and landed in the gorge. But close to I saw that they were all locked and interlocked as if embedded in concrete. It was dangerous to walk over them.

It was difficult to decide what should be done. One could wait until the next monsoon. The thousands of tons of water might dislodge them, but then another three to five thousand logs would be arriving with it. It was too dangerous a gamble. The block might be worse than ever.

137

One could blast, but I didn't like the idea of blasting. Even if it was merely superstition and not common sense given a divine sanction, I did not like to run counter to it. After all, one man's superstition is another's religion. "Try your elephants, Gerry," I said, "but the less said, the less discussed, the less even thought, the better." I found him ten tuskers. Then, remembering that ten was an unlucky number, I reduced it to nine; and I included among them Bandoola, whom I was sure the Nats loved.

The Burmese on the job were pessimistic. "The Nats will not let the logs go," they said; "if you anger them there will be tragedy."

But Gerry was young. He was strong. He was my ideal of a God-loving, God-fearing young man. He thought the Burmese Buddhists were pagans and that I was little better, because I respected their beliefs. He got to work with his tuskers and reported that they had loosened the jam. "But I need more," he wrote, "if I'm to finish before the monsoon. If they were all like Bandoola, it would be all right. He's the only one who will walk over the logs feeling his weight. When one creaks, he backs off it, because it needs moving. It's the unsteady ones which are causing the jam, not the dead-weight ones."

But I could not give him any more tuskers. When the early showers of the rainy season broke, I had to withdraw even the elephants he had. But Gerry was not satisfied to leave it to the monsoons, or the Nats, or both, to work things out between them for better or for worse. There were two enormous logs of over fifty feet in length, key logs and impossible for elephants to move. In company with a dangerous atheist, Soo Lin, Gerry Dawson planned to free them with dynamite, or datimiteo as the Burmans call it.

They made a bamboo raft and crossed a pool to the base of what remained of the jam. There they placed their charges with long fuses and made their get-away. The elephant men in the neighbourhood, who might no longer have been in the neighbourhood if they had known that dynamite was to be used, told me later that it was as if a thunderbolt had fallen and then an earthquake had crumbled in the sides of the gorge.

The dynamite shifted the whole balance of the logs. They collapsed in a sort of avalanche. But the loose overhanging rocks in the gorge collapsed also. Long before the elephant men arrived they could hear Soo Lin calling for help at the top of his voice.

What happened no one ever knew exactly, but the whole of Gerry's left forearm and wrist had been flattened to pulp. Gerry looked at it and pointed to Soo Lin's heavy jungle-knife. "Cut it off," he said, "quick."

Soo Linn struck as hard as he could. But he failed to amputate the hand. Gerry fainted. By the time the men had carried him out of the gorge to the top of the cliff, he had recovered sufficiently to ask for a small stone and a short stick. With his right hand and the help of his men he applied a tourniquet inside his biceps and secured it. "Get me to main river headquarters," he said; "quick as you can." Then he fainted again.

For four days and four nights his men carried him on a bamboo stretcher. They averaged four miles an hour and they doped him with opium the whole way. The tourniquet was never released.

When they arrived at that small riverine station, the one and only doctor, an Indian, was on tour. The only European was a civil policeman, the only nurse an English-speaking Karen girl of nineteen. She did all she could. She sent for the policeman. She removed the tourniquet and made Gerry as comfortable as she knew how.

It was obvious to both of them that an operation was immediately necessary. But who could operate? The policeman remembered that the Indian Sikh who was orderly to the police mules had some amateur veterinary knowledge. He summoned the man and ordered him to perform the operation. The nurse gave the anæsthetic and the policeman, holding a surgical book in his hand, supervised and accepted responsibility.

Frantic telegrams had been sent to summon medical help from Sagaing and Mandalay, but it was impossible to expect anyone until next day.

All things considered, the operation was a remarkable feat. The Sikh amputated above the pulped wrist.

When Gerry came round, he seemed in good shape and immediately asked to see Ma Kin and Shan Ma, two Shan girls, who would be found living in the servants quarters of his bungalow.

They were two sisters, one nineteen and the other seventeen. Both of them were proud and beautiful. Gerry had fallen in love with the elder girl in a small Shan village beyond the Shweli and had asked her to come to live with him as his mistress. She had accepted only on condition that her young sister should come with her and be his second mistress.

It was a peculiar household, because Gerry was passionately in love with them both and they both worshipped the ground he walked on. I knew that the Chinese ideograph for "trouble" represents two women under one roof. But under Gerry's roof they stood for "harmony." As one of his greatest friends, I was in his confidence and he once told me that the reason why Ma Kin wanted her sister to share him was because of the Shan belief that if two sisters were shared there would be no children, whereas if she were his sole mistress she would bear him children, and that would mean separation from him and perhaps the loss of his love.

The two sisters came to see him and he put on such a front while talking to them that they left without realising how dangerously ill he was.

The next morning a qualified Indian doctor arrived from Sagaing. He examined Gerry, congratulated the unfortunate Sikh on what he had done but announced that an immediate operation was necessary higher up the arm.

Gerry had scarcely come round when an Anglo-Indian doctor arrived from Mandalay. The two doctors had a consultation and it was decided that a third operation was necessary, to amputate to a short butt below the shoulder. As a result of the tourniquet not being released, gangrene had set in.

Finally Doc Harry arrived. He was one of those heaven-sent European doctors who had handled cases of every conceivable sort amongst jungle assistants, blackwater fever, hydrophobia, and enteric with every possible complication. His name was already a legend for miraculous cures.

Doc Harry examined him and then he shook his head. "I'm sorry, Gerry," he said. "There's nothing I can do now. It's too late. You'd better tell those girls of yours."

When Gerry told them, they burst into tears. "Why do you cry?" he said. "It's I who am going to die, not you." He patted their heads with his remaining hand. They went away, grief-stricken and yet quiet with that acceptance of the inevitable peculiar to the Orient.

Then Gerry turned to Doc Harry and asked if he might see the others, the policeman, the senior Forest man and the other doctors. They came in with long faces, but Gerry grinned. "There are two bottles of warm champagne in the club," he said; "let's have a drink; and to hell with this arm and Wabobin."

The party lasted ten minutes or so. His eyelids began to droop and Doc Harry nodded to the others to go out. "Time you had a sleep now, old boy." Gerry leaned back on his pillows, his legs propped higher than his head. "I shall sleep all right, doc," he said, "and I shall dream of the happiest twenty-nine years of life a man ever had."

I expected that the death of Gerry would strengthen the belief in the Nats of Wabobin. But I was wrong. He had lost his life, but he had cleared the gorge of that enormous timber stack. When the monsoon came, the floods came thundering down and with that monstrous load of timber they swept away the superstition attaching to the gorge. For years after that the logs passed through without a hitch and the Burmans worked without fear.

Perhaps when thirty years from now the area is worked again, the superstition will have revived. The place is eerie enough to play upon man's primitive fears. But it is most unlikely that there will be another Gerry Dawson to break down those fears.

Gerry, I think, must have had the premonition that he would die young. He had commuted his pension and in his will he left his capital to the two sisters. It fell to me to pay these young girls some time later. They seemed to be happy and resigned. Though they were still young and beautiful, they were contented to be Gerry Dawson's widows. Taking the money, they returned to their home to live with his memory.

While he was working in the Wabobin Gorge, Gerry kept his monthly diaries. After his death I read them through again. They were full of praise for Bandoola. His descriptions of Bandoola climbing the enormous stack of jammed timber made me realise what a tremendous achievement the unblocking of the gorge had been. Then as I read, I realised something which had never occurred to me before. Despite the fun which Gerry poured on the superstition of the anger of the Nats, he half-believed in it; but the victim all the time he suspected would be Bandoola, not himself.

No one who works in the jungle calculates on a ripe old age as a near-certainty. But Gerry's sense of death at his elbow, his philosophy of "Eat, drink and be merry," seems to me to date from the time of Paddy's death. Paddy was his greatest friend. He was given that name, not because he was Irish—he was not—but because he had a lock of hair which stood up from his head like the spray of feathers rising from the head of the egret or "paddy-bird." He had a habit of stroking it down with his hand, when he was reading, drinking or talking, one or more of which he was doing most of the time. But stroking made no difference. For a moment it would stick down, then up it sprang again.

Paddy was a very trusting person, even after he woke

up one morning to find that during the night someone had made off with his specie box containing fifteen thousand rupees.

The strange thing about the robbery was that Paddy and his dog had heard nothing. On the strength of this the police, to whom the matter was reported, arrested Paddy's head servant. He was charged and tried but the case was dismissed on the grounds that the evidence was insufficient.

Paddy was quite sure that the servant was innocent; but he replaced him while he was awaiting trial and his friends urged that it would be folly to re-engage a man who, though he had not been proved guilty, had at the same time failed to establish his innocence. That was the logic of common sense; but Paddy had a strong sense of justice. After a year he sought the man out and asked him to come back as head servant. The Burman was deeply touched at this sign of trust and for some years he served him with great devotion.

Then one day a confidential letter from the police arrived in Paddy's mail. It was seen by an English-speaking Burmese timber clerk, who immediately warned the head servant that the case had not been closed and suggested that the reason why Paddy had taken him back was to keep him under observation. The clerk, I imagine, thought that given this warning the head servant would be off.

Not a bit of it. The head servant said he was innocent and he saw no reason why he should give up a good job, just because the police were asking a few more questions. He appeared calm and unworried. He continued with Paddy in the usual way, but his mind was becoming unbalanced by worry as to what Paddy would reply.

The next morning he took Paddy's tea into his tent at dawn as usual and finding him asleep he tried to kill him with a large jungle-knife. The wounds he gave were mortal, but Paddy had time to scream for help before he died. The uproar woke the camp but the head servant grabbed a loaded shot-gun from under Paddy's bed and killed an old Burmese cook who came running to the rescue.

The servant got away and with a hue and cry behind him he made his way through the jungle to the village monastery, where he sought asylum and confessed to the priest. Having done so, he committed suicide, a thing almost unknown in Burma.

It was a curious tragedy of good intentions. There is no doubt that it was the servant who had stolen the money from the specie box. Everything would have ended comparatively happily if Paddy hadn't been such a good man. "The trouble about him," Gerry Dawson once said, "was that he was too good to live." In a way, Gerry was speaking his own epitaph.

CHAPTER TEN

ELEPHANT ITCH

WHEN I went into the jungle for the first time, I had highly-coloured ideas of man-eating tigers and charging wild tusker elephants. But after a comparatively short time I came to realise that the wild beasts of the jungle were not my natural enemies. They had no desire to attack me and I had no desire to attack them. (Big-game shooting, for all its excitement and skill, is, I am sure, at bottom the product of fear, the desire to blaze away at something in order to kill one's own fear.)

I do not mean that I ever lost my fear when I was in the jungle. No one but a fool could boast of such a thing. But I came to see that the things to be afraid of were not wild beasts, but the climate during the monsoon season and the repulsive creatures that flourished in the rains: the black silent anopheline mosquito

147

which carried malaria, the hookworm burrowing through the ankles and passing through the bloodstream to make its home in the upper intestines, the leeches on the dripping leaves and the tinea lurking in the mud.

The Burmans called this tinea Sin Wai, which being translated means Elephant Itch, or Elephant Scratch; the two being maddeningly synonymous. It was, alas! not confined to elephants, though they were the principal carriers, merely because of their weight and size. In the rainy season the elephant-tracks were churned into deep quagmires impregnated with Sin Wai. And of course the more years a forest area was worked, the worse it grew.

The elephants were more affected on the inner side of the hind-ankles than on the fore, as the skin there is not so serrated or tough. I have known elephants kick themselves raw by continuous scratching with their hind-feet. They seemed, however, to find some relief in standing in water.

Human beings and dogs become infected with Sin Wai through contact with the mud of the elephant-tracks. Slow and wearisome though these were to us, there was no other way in many places because the jungle was so dense. It only affected those parts of the body which came in contact with the foul mud, the legs up to the knees in the case of human beings, but in the case of dogs the whole under-belly also.

I had recently been given a liver-and-white springer

puppy six months old, named Chili. It was not a breed of dog I would have chosen for the jungle, but the man who gave her to me insisted that she would take the place of a dog I had lost from hookworm. Chili was very well bred and had the makings of a good gun-dog, obedient, bright, intelligent and with a good nose. When dry and brushed, her coat was silky and very pleasant in its markings. On the march or at exercise she was active and alert, but when that was over she curled up and went to sleep as if she was interested in nothing but the familiar and unfamiliar scents of the jungle.

During the rainy season one always had to take precautions against Sin Wai. The one hope lay in prevention. The Burman oozies used to urinate over their feet and ankles as their only preventative—even when in later years we used to issue them with a specially prepared ointment of methylene blue. It was messy to apply, and nothing would convince the oozie that it was more effective than his own urine and really not so messy.

I myself laced antiseptic with my hot washing-water, and after I had finished, though I never believed in washing dogs as a general rule, I would wash Chili free of the stinking mud that clung to her coat.

These precautions sufficed at the beginning. But then we got a bout of perfect Sin Wai weather. It rained very heavily for some days and then, when the tracks were deep in mud, the sun came out in spells to hatch the thing.

It all began on the same day. As we came into camp, we all started to scratch, the elephants, the oozies, the camp servants, Chili and I. At first small vesicles appeared on the skin, very irritating but not very angry in appearance. I smeared vaseline over my feet and ankles and treated Chili in the same way. For a long time I could not sleep, tired though I was; and when at last I did go to sleep, I continued to scratch the ankle of one foot with the sole of the other.

If we could have got out of the jungle, perhaps we could have cleared it up. But the trouble was that every day we became reinfected. The skin became more and more inflamed. Sleep became impossible. I tried pricking the vesicles in the early stages with a needle dipped in pure carbolic, hoping that the burn would either kill the bug or stop the irritation. But it gave no relief.

I knew the course which this hideous thing would take. Within a week, ulcers developed in some places on my calves. In sympathetic reaction the glands in my groins had swollen to the size of fists. It was impossible to stop scratching for a moment, impossible, even with the aid of whisky, to gain any sleep. The only thing that took my mind off my own irritation was the sight of poor Chili. She had scratched herself raw, and while I doctored her I had no time to think of myself.

I was able to give her some relief with baths of hot oatmeal-water prepared from Quaker Oats. But the time came when the last tin of Quaker Oats was empty. The Burmans recommended water in which fresh fish had been washed, but that proved useless. I had run out of vaseline long ago.

I was desperate. I had tried bandaging her toes to prevent the damage caused by her frenzied scratching. I had even tied her legs, only to release them again as the remedy seemed crueller even than letting her scratch herself to death. For the same reason I could not chain her.

I was in a high fever; my general weakness brought the malaria back. For a moment I dozed, scratching the right sole against the left ankle, right ankle against left sole. Suddenly there was a yelp. Chili had sprung from the floor of the hut, and as I opened my eyes she was out in a tropical downpour and the stinking mud. I went on to the veranda and called, "Chili! Chili!" I was in no state to follow her. I called again and again. But she was gone into the darkness and the insistent rain.

I thought, "She's gone to kill herself," remembering Tag's spaniel who for weeks was in agony with a bowel tumour. I persuaded Tag there was no hope of cure and to save him the grief of doing it I offered to put the bitch out of her pain. "All right," he said, "do it after breakfast." But when we looked for her after breakfast, she was gone, and though we hunted for her all day with a whole camp of men, we never found her. I thought that Chili had gone the same way as Tag's spaniel. I was very sorry, but I was too weak to do anything but yell for her.

When at last she did not come, I went back and lay down on my bed. My weeping sores ached and I was shivering with fever. Chili's going made up my mind for me. It had been raining for forty-eight hours. The river was in torrential spate. But I had to get out.

That was easier decided than done. This camp of Po Toke's was five marches to the nearest river navigable by country boat or dug-out; five marches through rain-sodden jungle along game-tracks knee-deep in mud. And even when I got there, there were the Yoo Rapids between me and the main river where I must go to rest up. In these rains the Yoo Rapids would be impassable. I could only pray that by the time I reached the river the floods would have subsided.

I lay thinking on my bed. Planning to move took my mind at least for the moment off the agonies of the flesh. I should have to go by elephant. But no calf elephant could cross those torrents rushing over boulder-strewn beds. Only a fully grown animal could keep its foothold. I thought of Bandoola, but it was Po Toke who suggested next morning that Bandoola should carry me.

I found that morning that I could no longer stand. I

had to be lifted into Bandoola's cane "kah." Before leaving, my men searched for any sign of Chili, but there was none. I prayed for her sake that she was already dead.

Each stage of that agonising trek was about ten miles. At every step Bandoola sank two or three feet deep into the mud. Each foot he lifted made a loud sucking noise and even his gigantic powers were sorely taxed.

Most of the time I was delirious. I remember in a moment of lucidity suddenly realising that we were crossing a torrent of chocolate-coloured water, against which Bandoola was leaning his weight so far over that I was nearly falling out. But the great elephant knew what he was doing. His massive head and tusks ploughed a passage through the water like the nose of a submarine. Riding on his powerful back brought home my own fragility.

I was unconscious when we reached the hut on the Yoo River, where in happier seasons I had grown huge bushes of bougainvillea. All I knew was that I was lying on my camp-bed, that my swollen groins had not burst, that the agony of the elephant's back was over. Beyond this Bandoola could be of no more assistance.

Propped on my camp-bed I could see the river. It was in full flood. Branches were torn from the boles of trees and carried off. Two large country dug-out boats arrived from up river and stopped. Ten miles below the rapids started, and it was suicide to try to shoot them. I was trapped. I would have to cure myself here.

I called for two empty kerosene-tins and had these filled with water as hot as I could possibly bear on my ulcerous legs. The discharge from the sores oozed down like black treacle and the relief was such that I was able to endure the pain in my groins for as long as a quarter of an hour before collapsing on my bed again.

After two days the swelling in the groins had somewhat lessened. But the strain had brought on severe malaria. The floods continued and I was no nearer help. I was too weak, too giddy in the head to care any longer. My servants came to me and suggested that the only way out would to be march on elephant again to the main river. It was virgin forest and it would take at least ten marches, hacking our way through. I shook my head. Another ten days on Bandoola's back would kill me; and if I was to die I preferred to die on my camp-bed beside the Yoo River. They tried to persuade me, but they were pleased when I was firm. If we got out at all, then we would get out on the river.

It was the last decision I took, for soon after that a third dug-out came down the river. And in it was one of the bravest and maddest forest men I ever knew, Colin Kayem. This is not the place for me to tell how Colin swam for two miles under a mountain looking for the reason why his teak-logs would not travel down a subterranean river. That is a story I shall tell some other time. Nor can I ever explain what possessed him to blue all his savings he had accumulated towards the enjoyment of one leave, on the invention and patenting of a form of head protection which should supersede the solar topee in the dry season and the umbrella during the monsoons. It was, I understand, a miniature umbrella-shaped contraption, held over the head by supports which strapped under the arms. It would have been quite practicable for jungle use provided that the jungle had been cleared.

Colin Kayem was, like myself, fleeing from the torrential rains and had put in to wait till the floods subsided and he could shoot the rapids. "Thank God, you're here," I said, and with that I resigned all responsibility. If it had not been for him, it is most unlikely that I should be alive to write this narrative.

He did not trouble to take my temperature. He had only to ask my servants a few questions to know that it was malaria, not typhus or enteric. For a whole night he dressed and drained my sores of the venom. By dawn he had me nearer normal than I had been for ten days.

Then he shocked me by saying. "We're getting out of this bloody hole. I'm making up a crew of three volunteer boatmen to shoot the rapids." He was a wonderful man. He could make the impossible sound as easy as winking. "I don't mind," I said; "anything you say."

I was carried down to the dug-out and placed in a

deck-chair, which just fitted the beam. There was no more talk of volunteers. It was "You and you" to the oarsmen, "And you," to a paddle-rudder helmsman. "I'll take the pole in the bows," Kayem said, "just in case we lose our way."

Hearing the "volunteers" muttering, Kayem turned on them. "What's all the talk about?" he said quietly in Burmese. "D'you think I'd risk it if I didn't know we could do it? There's only one man who'll drown if we capsize. And he's game to go, even if he *is* ill."

Under my canopy of a waterproof sheet and hidden from view, I had to smile for the first time in days. It was a perfect Kayem argument, though I wasn't sure whether it was the Kayem who swam under the mountain or the Kayem who invented the sunshade-umbrella.

Two of my servants made up the boat-load. We cast off from the bank. My elephant men who had carried me down shouted and cheered. I wondered how many of them were really saying good-bye.

The muddy brown water, built up above the rapids, was flowing quite silently, though at speed in the centre. We began by moving upstream, while the two oarsmen got into position facing me, the helmsman grasped his fixed paddle-rudder and planted his feet firmly so that he would not be thrown overboard. In the bows Kayem wielded a long wabo pole fitted with a spike at one end.

The oars creaked in their rope runnels. The bow was taken by the current and as the helmsman shouted

"We can pull in at Kyauth Ngapun to see what the rapids are doing" we swung out and down and away.

For an hour we had fair going. The only warning of the river's commotion was that every now and again it vomited beneath us and lifted us, before it flattened out like a great blister of oil.

Once as we were passing, a high bank fell, and a dozen fully-grown trees crashed into the river, sending a bore of water a foot high broadside at us and rocking the boat perilously. To me the excitement was a tonic. I asked to have the canopy removed.

"Keep well out on the bends," yelled the helmsman.

We were going all out now. When we got into fast water, the oarsmen had to pull like mad to give us steering way. At the mouth of the Ngapyaw, a tributary on the right bank which was also in spate, we ran into rough water. But the dug-out rode nicely and we soon settled down.

As we neared the Ngapun rapid the roar became terrific. But Kayem gave them no chance to pull in. He started singing the Burmese boat song "Hey Los! Hey Los!" as they strained and pulled at their oars. The helmsman, who was the owner of the boat, took it up and headed us straight for the broken water. Suddenly we were drawn into it and caught and tossed as helpless as a cork. Desperately the oarsmen struggled to keep her head on. Then with the waves dashing over the sides we tore ahead through the channel and we were down, baling out the water we had shipped in the comparative calm of the eddying pool below.

The Ngapun rapid was the first but by no means the worst. Kayem drove us on to take the next, the main Yoo River rapids, without a pause. I had shot these many times before in normal conditions, but never without anxiety even then. They were devils even in the best of weathers. No one had ever tried to shoot them in floods like these; if anyone else had tried to do it, I would have said it was suicidal. But Kayem, who had been the runner-up for the Diamond Sculls, was as good a waterman as he was a swimmer: and his was the sort of recklessness that triumphs.

I lay back in my deck-chair, too weak to worry but not too weak to picture what lay ahead, the five consecutive rapids and at the bottom of the last the sheer cliff against which the river took a right-angled bend, forming at its base a gaping whirlpool.

We could hear the rapids from a long way off. At first it sounded like a gentle murmur, then like the ground-swell off the Cornish coast. As we rounded each bend the sound grew louder and louder, at the same time deepening in tone. As we took the last bend it struck us so loud that it seemed as if it were an entirely new noise, like thunder echoing through the dense jungles and the surrounding hills. At the same moment it started to rain again.

Kayem had stripped to the waist. He stood in the

bows with his powerful rounded shoulders braced, his spiked pole raised as if in readiness to meet some charging monster. No one spoke. No orders were given. The helmsman had it all in his hands.

Looking ahead I saw this hellish broken water with spray flying. Huge jagged rocks like great basking sharks stood out on the side of the channel towards which we were heading. There was no changing course. The flood took our dug-out and drove it forward with the speed of an outboard motor. Our bows hit the first wave of broken water. Kayem disappeared from sight in a cloud of spray. For a moment I thought that we were going to submerge like a submarine. But the bows rose and Kayem appeared in sight again. The water we shipped poured into the well and half-drowned me. But the crew was intact and the two oarsmen rowing like mad still held our way.

The waves appeared to tear past us upstream, high above the level of my head. Perhaps this wasn't an illusion created by our speed. Perhaps the downward plunging of the flood-water produced a surface backwash. I don't know. All I know is that it was one of the most alarming experiences of my life, momently expecting that we should be submerged or else turned turtle by a hidden rock or dashed to splinters against a boulder.

Curiously all the time, as though the rapids themselves were not alarming enough, I was thinking, "but even if we get down, we shall hit that cliff, going at this speed."

We shot forward out of the broken water. Kayem raised his pole to fend us off from the cliff, but with a perfect timing the helmsman turned his paddle-rudder. The craft heeled over. We missed the rock by feet and Kayem struck it a powerful blow, to give us headway. But it was not enough. We had lost the race of water and the current of the outer rim of the whirlpool had caught us. "Swai! Swai! Swai!" yelled the helmsman. "Pull! Pull! Pull!"

But all the pulling in the world could not bring us back into the main current. We swung drifting sideways around the outer ring of the vortex, part of the flotsam, the floating branches making the slow corkscrew circuits to the sucking centre. I looked desperately for something which I might clutch to save myself before the dug-out took a dive and spin below. Then suddenly our craft swung out again into the outer circle.

As we came to the down-river edge, the two oarsmen pulled like demons. Kayem, leaning from the bows, tried to dangle his pole in the race, hoping that the extra pull would be enough to draw us out of that strong circle of water. But there was not enough on the smooth pole to grip. Back and around we swung.

We circled nineteen times, no longer now drawn towards the centre. We had strength enough to keep on the periphery, but not the strength to break away. For an hour this went on, with the dug-out sometimes a little nearer the centre and sometimes a little nearer the rim. It began to look as if it might go on forever.

Then Kayem fastened a groundsheet to the end of his pole, and each time we came down-river he made a cast into the race, the oarsmen pulling with all their strength. One moment we were going with the whirlpool; the next we were plucked like a twig and carried broadside on down the race.

As the helmsman straightened up, Kayem turned round and grinned at me. "Don't worry, old boy," he said. "You'll see Paris again."

I grinned in answer and then, the suspense over, I leaned back and went to sleep. I did not realise until later quite how ill I was.

CHAPTER ELEVEN

A MIXED BAG

IT was almost Christmas before I was fit for the jungle
again. I wanted to get back in time to supervise the
crossing of the Upper Chindwin River by thirty-five of
my elephants. Fortunately Willie, who from being my
old taskmaster had become a very good friend, had sole
use of the company's stern-wheel paddle-launch. He
was doing his farewell trip on tour up-country, and
suggested that we should combine his Christmas shoot
with an official trip to watch the river-crossing.

The paddle-launch was a luxury ship compared with
the craft in which Willie and I had played Northern
Farmer with the oilmen and the missionary. A miniature showboat with spotless white paint, a black stack,
an upper deck with four comfortable cabins amidships,
saloons fore and aft and adequate deck-space for
exercise.

There were two other guests: Millie the connoisseur of elephant-droppings under whom I had served in my second year, and a young man called Tony. Tony was handsome and immaculate. Every article of his jungle kit had been selected with care at home. His shooting-stick came from Swaine and Adeney, his topee from Hawkes, his hair tonic from Truefitts, his shorts and shirts were tailored by Threshers. With a little make-up, he could in fact have walked straight on to a film-set to play the part of a white man in the jungle. He was very amusing company, but he was deeply in love with a very beautiful girl; and it was quite plain even then that in the tug-of-war between the jungle and the girl, the girl would win.

As soon as Tony and I boarded the launch, it was clear that though elsewhere folk might be waiting till Christmas Day came in three days' time, Christmas had come aboard the launch several hours before. Willie and Millie had got a start on us, but as we went full steam ahead, Tony and I rapidly caught them up.

Willie made us all help with the decorations. He had a Wensleydale cheese the size of a wheel, doctored to perfection and swathed in damp muslin. All drinks for cooling were slung in baskets over the stern so that the paddle should keep them sprayed. The champagne at lunch was followed by Napoleon brandy. There were real crackers, and in place of Burmese cheroots, Coronas. Yes, Christmas started early that year.

That evening we pulled up at four o'clock and shot until dusk over a lake where ducks and geese abounded. It was such shooting that no one could mention it to those who talk of wild-fowling on the East coast of England, for fear of being written down a liar. When we got back it took us an hour to sort and classify our bag.

It was Christmas day for three days, and on the real Christmas Eve we came to the fords where the elephants were to cross. They were all congregated in a central camp. Early on Christmas morning Willie inspected them. Then they were released and the elephant men were impressed to act as beaters for the day. There was beat after beat of jungle fowl, sky-high birds; a bag that day of ninety-two and three barking deer.

We went back to the launch and had hot baths and then a Christmas dinner unequalled on any table in the land. We were all satisfied and tired. Such a day and night made us forget such things as monsoons, mud, leeches and malaria.

I ventured to hint that it was bedtime. Tomorrow the elephants had to cross, and they were my responsibility. It was very quiet. There was only the low hum of the generator which provided us with the luxury of electric light. Perhaps just a nightcap, I thought, and then a perfect sleep to end a perfect day.

Suddenly Willie called for Po Pyan, his head-servant, who appeared from the darkness of Willie's cabin where he had been squatting silently waiting to put Willie to bed, as he had done every night for the last fifteen years. "Clear the table," Willie said in Burmese, and then, turning to us, "Let's make it a *real* Christmas and play bridge."

"No," said Tony; "you mean snapdragon."

"No," corrected Millie. "Bed is what you mean."

I got up and fetched the cards. I knew Willie. If Willie said bridge, then bridge it would be.

It was serious bridge, perhaps even "solemn" would be a better word to describe it. There were no post-mortems, not a word spoken in anger. There was no need to speak, for Willie, whose partner I was, could express himself perfectly by merely looking.

The hours flowed past as smoothly as the river beneath us and the whisky down our throats. How many bottles were emptied I do not know; but the moment a glass was empty Po Pyan refilled it without being bidden.

We had reached that stage of utter fatigue when even the thought of getting up to go to bed is an effort. The fifth rubber dragged interminably on. But at last there was a hand which stood a fair chance of making game, rubber and bed. We were all left with three cards as Willie collected a trick from the table and laid it neatly in line with our tricks. We waited for him to lead. He sighed deeply. His left hand holding his cards flopped with them face downwards on the table, his half-smoked cigar fell from the fingers of the other hand to the deck. His chin sagged on to his chest. He was out.

We leant back in our chairs and stared at each other without speaking. Po Pyan had disappeared. The sound of the water lapping the sides of the launch seemed to become very loud.

We sat like this for some minutes. I had a mind to say, "What a pity he isn't dummy!" but I saw the intense gravity of Millie's face. He bent down and tried to look up at Willie. Willie was absolutely still. No sign of the heavy breathing of a man who has passed out. Looking very white, Millie rose from his chair and made away from the aft saloon where we had been playing in the direction of the fore saloon. Tony shrugged his shoulders, held up the palms of his hands and then followed Millie on tiptoe.

I didn't know what to do. I had often seen Willie pass out, but never quite like this. There was only one way of describing his state. Flat out. I got up and followed them.

They turned as I came into the fore saloon. I was shocked. Millie was as white as a sheet. Tony looked terrible. I tried to smile but I drew no smile from them.

"It's terrible," Millie said, "heart failure. I always knew it."

"Don't be ridiculous," I said. "I've seen him pass out dozens of times before."

"I've watched him passing out for thirty years," said Millie, "but never like this."

"I'm new to all this," Tony said, "but I must say I didn't like that sigh; and did you see his colour? Ghastly."

I did not feel by any means the optimism I pretended. It was so horribly appropriate an end, the cheese and crackers, the launch and Christmas dinner in the jungle. "Well, you're senior, Millie," I said. "You go back and shake him and see."

"I shall do nothing of the sort," Millie answered sharply. "Nothing would induce me to do such a thing. After all, you should know him best. And besides, it's your forest he's visiting."

"As a matter of fact," I said, turning to Tony, "I think you ought to go, old boy. After all, he's almost a stranger to you. You'd find it less of a shock than we would."

Tony hesitated as he tapped a cigarette on his gold cigarette-case. But Millie broke in: "That's unfair to Tony. It's your duty and you know it."

As I went out, I bowed to them both. "A madly happy Christmas to you!" I said, smiling; but my smile cannot have been convincing, because they did not smile back.

Willie was in exactly the same position as when I had left him. His cigar, still burning, was marking the deck. I picked it up and placed it on the ash-tray beside him.

A MIXED BAG

As I did so, I noticed the bald patch on the top of his head. It had lost its sunburn. It looked as white as a bladder of lard and as cold.

There was no sign of life in the man and yet I could not touch him. If I tried to feel his pulse, I thought, he might wake up and accuse me of looking at his cards. Or he might not wake up.

Suddenly I realised that I deeply loved Willie, from whom I had learnt so much of hardness and kindness. My heart grew cold with fear at the thought of him dead. I wanted to continue the illusion that he was living a little longer. I sat down in my chair opposite him with my three unplayed cards face down on the table before me. I picked up my glass and drank my whisky slowly, looking all the time at his ghastly face, his slumped inanimate body.

As I put down my glass, despite my care it clinked against an ash-tray; it was like a touch of magic. His set lips fluttered to a smile, as if he was still in some dream, and then, coming fully awake, he looked up. He looked at me blearily, then at the empty chairs. He turned his three cards face upwards on the table. "Game and rubber!" he said. "I knew you wouldn't leave me, partner." He heaved himself up and staggered the ten paces to his cabin. As he opened the door, I saw Po Pyan appear out of the darkness and catch him in his arms.

At dawn a few hours later, very few, I was awakened

by Willie with a glass of black velvet in his hand, a fifty-fifty mixture of champagne and stout. "You had rather a thick night, partner," he said, "you'll probably need this to see those elephants across."

At breakfast there was no mention of the night before. Willie, I noticed, looked far more alive than any of us.

The air was cold and there was a heavy morning dew. A river mist hung over the water. Occasionally the tops of the forest trees on the opposite bank appeared above the mist like a mirage, reminding me of the work ahead.

It was not going to be an easy crossing. The river at this point was about a mile wide. It was divided in the centre by a long spit of sand and shingle. Both of the two channels thus formed were fordable, but in the centres there were two considerable swims. With thirty-five elephants making the crossing, they would be scattered by the time they reached the other side, some of them drifting as much as half a mile downstream.

I was far more anxious than I appeared to be when at ten o'clock I left the launch. But the only one of them I deceived was young Tony. "We'll be along at noon," Willie shouted; "you won't get them started before then."

U San Din, a very old man, was in charge of the whole herd, which was divided into five sections of seven, each under their respective Singaungs. Being all fully grown, they appeared an enormous herd stretched out along the low bank of kaing grass, and the shingly foreshore.

The mist was rising, but the water and the air were still cold. There was no hope of persuading the animals or the men to enter the water before the heat of the day. But it was possible to show the elephants, particularly those who had swum rivers before, what was afoot. The families of the elephant men crossed first in canoes, three or four at a time. Then the elephant gear was ferried over in larger dug-outs.

None of us had any idea which animal would lead. But we kept eight possibles lined up along the water's edge. Bandoola and all the other full-grown tuskers were kept far back from the river bank. Of those at the water's edge all were females except one, a large tuskless Hine who looked an unintelligent beast compared to the females.

U San Din shouted to the riders of the tuskers not to come near the water until all the others were swimming. Then he asked me to give the order to stop all talking. That was about two o'clock; after which I rejoined the others, who were sitting on the branch of an old tree stranded on the shingle.

In the silence the eight possible leaders entered the water as casually as if they were going for their daily scrub. The elephant riders turned in their seats and tested the surcingle ropes secured around the bodies of their elephants. These were life-lines which they could grip when they reached deep water. There was a general shuffling and at least a dozen elephants entered the water at various points. But though some of them went into deep water, not one would start to swim.

"What's all this I've heard about every herd of elephants having a leader?" Tony asked. "Can't see any ruddy leaders in this bunch."

Much to the amusement of Willie and Millie, I took Tony up sharply. "You're in the jungle to learn about elephants," I said. "Forget that muck you've read from shikaris who've never seen an elephant without killing him. You wait. You'll see this herd will follow a young female elephant as the wild ones do."

U San Din was being paddled up and down in a small dug-out canoe. One could almost feel him praying that something would happen as a start.

Then suddenly there was a commotion. A young female elephant came scuttling down the shingle, her rider working his feet behind her ears as if he was pedalling a low-gear bicycle. There was a tremendous splash as she entered the water. It grew less and deepened its note as she waded into deeper water. Suddenly she lunged forward into the channel. For a moment she disappeared, rider and all; then she rose with the buoyancy of a cork. She was afloat, swimming steadily towards the shingle island in mid-river. She tried to drift in the current and it was all that U San Din's paddlers could do to find a position below her and head her off.

The elephant had a lovely swimming action, a sort of slow lunging which totally immersed the rider every now and again as she dived. When he came up, he waved his hand to those behind.

Now one female followed after the other. It was like a herd of cattle in a summer meadow, suddenly following one goaded by a gadfly. They went out across the river in line ahead, launching into deep water like life-boats.

The sight was so marvellous that quite instinctively we all stood up to watch it. The young leader did not land on the shingle bank. The current carried her well below it, and the others followed in her course. Now the tuskers began to take off. Bandoola, by far the most massive, stood out even in the water. Soon every animal was away, strung out like gigantic corks on an invisible rope stretched from where we stood to a point on the far bank at least a mile below us. For this migration the elephants, who worked in teams and as individuals, suddenly became a herd as in the wild state, following the females.

That evening, U San Din came, on Willie's orders, with his five Singaungs to the launch so that we could congratulate them. "Isn't it extraordinary," Tony asked, "that the leader should be a young female, instead of a great tusker like Bandoola?"

Po Toke, though he certainly knew nothing of Tony's love-life, answered, "Well, Thakin, men will go where women go. But very often women will not go where men go. Why should elephants be different?"

Tony grew red.

Later that evening our peace and my holiday were broken into. A message came that Bandoola had killed his rider.

It was not an uncommon thing for an elephant on musth to kill an oozie. It is a professional hazard for the elephant-rider and in such cases we held no enquiry. That deep ungovernable rage which possesses the male elephant at such a time was accepted as part of his nature; and it was agreed that any oozie who was killed then had only himself to blame.

But Bandoola had not been on musth. It was apparently a wanton and unprovoked attack. Aung Bala, the oozie, had been adjusting Bandoola's fore-fetters, when tied to a tree. Suddenly the tusker gored him, then knelt his enormous weight upon him and finally with peculiar viciousness tossed his body from his reach with his tusks. If the killing of an oozie when on musth was justifiable homicide, this looked horribly like murder.

When I reached the camp, I tried to discover the facts from the Burmans. But Burmans regard such investigations as one of those western absurdities. Did they consider that Aung Bala had been careless? They shrugged their shoulders. Aung Bala was dead. No enquiry would bring him back to life.

I went to inspect Bandoola. He appeared completely

normal, except that he was fettered and attended by two spearmen, one of whom was Po Toke. It was strange, and to me rather tragic, to see Po Toke, who had struggled so hard to train this elephant without cruelty, taking up a position with a spear.

I treated Bandoola with circumspection as I had no desire to follow Aung Bala. But from as near as I dared approach, I could see no spear-marks or signs of ill-treatment on him. I told Po Toke to hold back each ear in turn, so that I could see if during the swimming Aung Bala had "kyooned" or hooked him. But there wasn't a mark. Bandoola seemed happy and contented, normal in every way as he munched at his fodder. The only thing which was abnormal, as I suddenly noticed, was the amount of his fodder: whole plantain trees, sugar-cane, bamboos, branches of nyaung.

Then I noticed another thing, which made me very suspicious. There were no droppings and yet no signs that Aung Bala had done any cleaning up around his charge. I walked round Bandoola, Po Toke following me with his eyes rather apprehensively. I turned on him suddenly. "Who gave Bandoola all this fodder?"

"Aung Bala, just before he was killed," said Po Toke. But a shade too quickly. I was sure that he was lying, and I walked away and went straight to Helaw village, about half a mile away, where U San Din had taken Aung Bala's body to the headman's house. Po Toke followed me, padding along slightly behind but not saying a word. We passed a number of elephants which had made the crossing. All of them had practically finished the fodder which their oozies had provided. This was one thing which I noticed; the other was that Po Toke saw that I noticed it.

At the steps of the headman's house, U San Din met me. "Dokha gyi (this is big trouble)," he said.

"You must expect big trouble from an elephant with an empty belly," I said. I looked at U San Din and I looked at Po Toke. I could see the shot had gone home. "You can go now, Po Toke," I said.

When he had gone, U San Din told me the story without reserve. Ma Pyoo, as I have said, had given Po Toke no children. For many years it had been their common sorrow. Now, either because he desperately wanted children or because Ma Pyoo's beauty had faded or perhaps for both these reasons, Po Toke had sent Ma Pyoo back to her village and taken to himself a second wife, a girl of sixteen. In this there was nothing contrary to the Buddhist religion. But it rarely happened among the Burmans of the jungle—it was more the practice of the wealthy people of the towns.

Po Toke himself did not feel easy about it. For two days before the river-crossing he had neglected all his duties as a Singaung. This would not have mattered much if Aung Bala had not been an opium-eater. U San Din admitted that for two days before the crossing Bandoola had been left chained to trees with little or no fodder except what was within his reach. The oozies, when I questioned them, stated that it was not two days but three.

When Aung Bala chained him again after crossing the river, Bandoola grew desperate. He tangled his chains and fetters trying to draw attention to his hunger. But instead of giving him more to eat, Aung Bala tried to untangle them; and then the captive elephant saw red.

It was Po Toke who had betrayed their negligence by trying to cover it with that enormous amount of fodder.

As I returned to the launch late that night, there were strange thoughts in my head. I remembered how during the rebellion I had felt that as a European I lived within a clearing in the clearing, that I didn't know what was going on in the minds of my oozies. I felt it again now. It is very hard to fix responsibility. Was the responsibility Aung Bala's entirely? I did not know till now that he was an opium-eater, and I should never know why. The break-up of Po Toke's marriage with Ma Pyoo, which I had envied for its apparent happiness, made Po Toke responsible for the tragedy. But then I remembered that during those two days of crisis, when Po Toke had dismissed the woman he had loved most and neglected the elephant who was his pride, I myself had been enjoying a protracted Christmas, shooting, eating and drinking to repletion.

Willie was waiting for me when I boarded the launch

and I told him what had happened, though not what I had been thinking. "It's up to you to dismiss Po Toke or not as you like," he said. "But I agree that you cannot brand Bandoola as a killer in his history sheet. If you do, you'll make him one soon enough."

So the killing did not go down in Bandoola's official record. There was no spearman attendant whose jabs would have goaded him into frenzy. But nothing that Willie or I or anybody else could do stopped tongues from wagging. Every oozie who had heard tell of Bandoola learned sometime or other, round a dying fire, that Bandoola had killed Aung Bala when he was not on musth, but not necessarily the reason why.

The next morning Po Toke came to plead with me for forgiveness. He was heartbroken. There was no need for him to feign contrition. It was easy enough for me to understand what had happened. It was not so easy to decide what to do. When one is in a high position of responsibility in the jungle, one has to trust everybody. I remembered what Willie had said to me after I had operated on the killer elephant's abscess. "You've got to look out for that man, Po Toke." I remembered Po Toke's sudden resignation, his overstaying of long leave. There was, now that he had dismissed Ma Pyoo, only one constant thing in his life: his devotion to Bandoola.

"I ought to dismiss you," I said, "but I don't want to do that. After what has happened to Aung Bala, I can't

M 177

employ you as a Singaung. But I'm willing to pay you the same wage, to be Bandoola's oozie."

"In the same camp?"

He was thinking of his "face."

"No, I will transfer you both."

Po Toke bowed his head in acceptance. The wage would enable him to keep his new wife. The charge of Bandoola was really all he cared about. His genius was for that elephant alone. To train him he had evolved a revolutionary technique but he was bored at using it on other elephants. A very simple man, he had three ambitions, to beget a son, to manage the greatest elephant in the forest, and to see his country independent. All three of them in the end were frustrated. The bitterest failure of them all was probably the first. Despite her youth his second wife never conceived. The marriage which was intended to prove Ma Pyoo's barrenness proved quite the opposite. Looking back, Po Toke must have been able to see no excuse for his negligence which killed Aung Bala.

CHAPTER TWELVE

THE POISON OF PO LONE

IN *Elephant Bill* I described how I was sent in charge of a party to explore the uninhabited forests of the Northern Andaman Islands. But I did not describe an incident arising out of that assignment, which was of lasting importance in my life.

There was only one thing which marred my excitement at the prospect of going to the Andaman Islands, and that was the future of my Alsatian, Molly Mia. I could not take her with me and though she was not, like Ba Sein, a dangerous animal, I was frightened that when separated from me she might pine. For she was as devoted to me as I was to her. Her devotion had become something of a by-word.

As I made my first move from the jungle, this question of Molly Mia occupied my thoughts. I think she realised it too, from the excess of affection which I lavished on her to cover up my imminent departure.

On one stage of my march out I met two Burmese foresters who told me that a man I knew, the Chief Conservator of Forests, was camped on my line of march in the Bwetgyi drainage where he had already shot one tiger and was remaining a few days in the hopes of another. I decided to descend upon his camp and spend the night with him.

His camp, the forester said, was not far away, and very soon, looking down, I saw him fishing in a stream. I went over and chatted with him. He seemed delighted to see me and asked me to pitch down with him on his camp; but to have my travelling elephants released down-river, so that they would not mix with his, which were upstream.

"See you later," I said and pushed on to his camp site. It was on the high bank of the river, and as I crossed it, I saw there were two tents instead of one. I was surprised because he had not mentioned that he had company, and rather disappointed because I was afraid I might not be able to talk as much about the North Andaman Islands as I had hoped.

I was in two minds about turning away when I saw a tall, slender girl in the clearing. She had seen me, and waved. There was no possibility of turning back.

I raised my Terai hat, a form of soft hatting made of double felt which I had copied from Willie, no one else having dared to copy him during his service.

This Terai hat was far more comfortable and practical than a solar topee. But as I crossed the clearing, it occurred to me that it might appear slightly ridiculous. I felt, I confess, rather shy.

"My name is Susan," she said, "my uncle's fishing somewhere," and she waved upstream. She seemed, reassuringly, as shy as I was. Or perhaps she was embarrassed at an unwelcome stranger? Or was it just my hat?

Molly Mia, who usually avoided strangers, ran across to her and allowed herself to be stroked.

"What a lovely dog," Susan said. "I know who you are, because I've heard all about Molly Mia." Molly Mia looked up at the sound of her name and her tongue hung out. "They say you're inseparable."

That we weren't inseparable I soon discovered. I've never seen anything like it. Molly Mia had never been handled by a woman in her life, but she attached herself immediately to Susan, completely ignoring me. When Susan went into her tent, Molly Mia followed. While we sat round the large log-fire, listening to the chief conservator's interminable angling yarns, Molly Mia crouched beside Susan's shapely legs.

At last, about midnight, the old boy took himself off, saying that he had to make arrangements about killing a tiger next day. As soon as he left, I realised how useful his long stories had been. I wanted to be with this young woman but I couldn't think of anything to say.

Merely to break the silence, I said, "If you'd like her, Susan, I'll give you Molly Mia."

She shook her head. "Let's share her," she suggested. "I'll look after her until you return from the Andamans."

That was a bargain as far as I was concerned. But I wondered how Molly Mia would feel about it. It might with luck be managed, I thought.

We stood up to say good-night, and as we went to our respective tents Molly Mia went not with me but with Susan.

The next morning I said to her, "You'd better keep Molly Mia on a leash when I go." I said good-bye to the dog, rather furtively hoping that there might be a bit of a scene, but Molly Mia merely wagged her tail. When I had gone about half a mile from the camp, I waited listening for the sound of the Alsatian crashing after me. But no, there was silence.

"Well," I said to myself, as I started off again, "if she's got Molly Mia when I get back, the only way I'll get her back will be to marry the girl."

And so it was. Susan and I were married on home leave and for our honeymoon we returned to the jungles.

I had achieved after eleven years hard work what had been my ambition when I first came to Burma and was working under Willie. I had found an English woman whose pleasure in the jungle was equal to my own.

Bruce Walker had taken his Burmese mistress, Willie had married the bottle. But there was this third possibility, and I believed that Susan and I would make a success of it.

But married life brought its changes. Soon after we came back to the jungle, I took a polo side from our up-country station Mawlaik to Monywa. This meant a three-day river-trip in the firm's launch down-river, a week's polo, and a voyage back. The heat was terrific in Monywa. We had struck a dry spell in the monsoon so hot that we had to play at six in the morning. This did not moderate the party spirit at the club and private houses on the night before. And I remember rising at half-past five and deciding that the only thing which would carry me through the game was a prairie oyster, the yolk of a raw egg doctored in a wineglass with vinegar, Worcester sauce, pepper, salt and mustard.

It was a bachelor habit; and though Susan disapproved, she agreed to make me one as I struggled to put on my polo-boots while a hundred little men with hammers seemed to be tapping on the inside of my skull.

Our host had provided us with a liberal supply of eggs the night before. She broke thirteen of them before she found a good one and when she had fixed the prairie oyster, she said, "You can play polo if you like, but I'm going back to bed."

The next day we reverted to evening play, and the

183

following morning I saw a bachelor party through the eyes of a married man. It was 6 a.m. and the tropical sun was already hot, when Susan woke me. She was at the veranda window. "Come and look," she said.

Very reluctantly I got up and went to the window. On the Chummery lawn they were still sitting where we had left them four hours before, with their pressure-lamps still alight under the blazing sun. One of them yawned, got up and carrying his lamp staggered home to bed. How many times the sun had risen on my bachelor parties and it was rather fun! But didn't it look frowsy from that veranda window! "Oh come on," I said, self-righteously, "let's go back to bed."

The monsoon broke again as we started back. The river rose and on the third day flood-water prevented us from navigating the Kalewa defile in daylight. But the Indian Serang assured us that it would be quite safe for us to steam up to Kalewa and tie up there for the night, because we had a powerful searchlight. Though the river was in spate no logs were moving.

The launch, with thirteen ponies on the lower deck and our polo party on the upper deck, made slow but steady progress up the defile against the swift current. The searchlight was trained on the rock wall of the defile, but every now and again it would be swung across the river to make sure that no timber was coming through.

It is always exciting to steam through a gorge, even in

daytime and with a slow-moving stream. We all stood leaning over the rails, watching the tear of the river swirling and breaking in little white waves which were caught by the searchlight, and towering above us the great cliffs either side, and over all the stars. It gave me a wonderful sense of man's mastery, the way we chugged along, steering by the searchlight on the cliff.

Then suddenly all lights went out. There was a sense of silence, even though the engines were still running. It was merely the generator which had failed.

The current at this point bore hard against one cliff, and amid the yells of the Indian crew I expected any moment to hear and feel the grind and crunching of the launch as in the darkness we smashed against the rock-face by which we had been steering.

I ran to get a lifebelt to give to Susan, thinking as I fumbled with it that we must untie the ponies, to give them at least a chance. If we struck, it would be a matter of minutes before we foundered. I got the lifebelt free and ran back, calling to Susan. But there was no answer. She seemed to have disappeared.

Suddenly the beam of a torch leaped out, lighting up the cliff-face towards which we were heading. The launch heeled over as the Serang swung her to starboard away from the rocks; and Susan, whose torch it was, made quickly for the bows, keeping the torch beam steady on the cliff. She had saved us from certain catastrophe.

But we were not out of danger. As we lost the guide of the cliff-face, there was the new risk of the current swinging our bows round.

Fortunately at that moment the lights came on again. An Indian fitter-engineer had gone straight to the trouble and rectified it.

We were all shaken by this incident; but at the same time I was reassured. Susan would be the only European woman in the station, and during the rainy season she would not be able to come with me on my tours. I had done my best to make the place comfortable. From the point of view of food and domestic service, her life might be considered easy. But there would be loneliness, and in times of sickness great responsibility. I knew now that I had married a woman of resource with a singular capacity for rising to a crisis.

Yet it was not very long before a crisis arose with which I feared she could not cope, since she was in ignorance of the danger.

Three days after our return to the station, we were all out touring our respective forest areas. To make the transition from bachelor to married life more peaceful, I had dismissed my old headquarters staff with one exception and engaged fresh staff, who would accept my wife's more ordered management of the household without question. The exception was Po Lone, to whom I had given leave when we went on our polo week and who was due back about a week after my departure on tour.

I thought that he might fit in with the new regime, and if he didn't, it would be time enough to dismiss him when I came back.

The hot dry spell we had enjoyed in Monywa was succeeded by particularly heavy monsoons. Jungle-touring was grim. I had been on tour about a month and had reached the camp where my old friends Bandoola and Po Toke were working, about three days' hard march from headquarters. I had hoped to receive mail here by jungle messenger. But there was none waiting for me when I arrived.

It was late evening. The rain ran off the small thatched huts in sheets. The creek, already half in spate, was still rising. Everything in the dense forest was drenched and dripping, all elephant and game tracks were reduced to quagmires. I felt very depressed. There seemed no chance of mail arriving that night. The Singaung of the camp was ill with what I suspected was beri-beri; two of the oozies were down with the same thing. Life was dreary, dismal and lonely; but all the same I had much to be thankful for, I thought, as I settled down to write my letters.

Aung Net left my hut and went to join my other servants. Aung Net was someone to be thankful for, a simple, loyal soul. He had come into my life in a strange way. One day I had been out shooting jungle fowl, when Aung Net, then a village boy of fifteen, came up to me excitedly with what I thought for a moment was a new-born baby leopard in his arms. It wasn't. It was a new-born puppy, a spaniel which must I suddenly realised be one of the litter of my spaniel bitch working in the cane-break with the beaters. She was a fanatic gun-dog, who put master, bird and gun above everything else. She had dropped her puppies one by one in intervals while she worked the cover.

I told Aung Net to look for others; and he found four more scattered over a wide area. If that wasn't the complete litter, at any rate it satisfied the mother. And I was so pleased with the boy that I asked him if he would like the job of looking after them. In this way began a service which was to last for twenty-two years. No man ever knew me better and I knew him as I knew no other Burman. He grew up with me almost as my son.

My thoughts were still of Aung Net when he returned, followed by the messenger San Pyoo. As he climbed the rickety bamboo ladder of my hut on stilts, he called "Sak yauk byee." Mail had come.

San Pyoo was stripped to the waist. His long hair was dripping wet and he looked dead beat. He dropped the mail-bag as if to say "I am here", but he did not speak.

"Is there any news?" I asked.

"No," he said, "but I met Bandoola down creek. I was frightened to cross at the rocky ford. That is why I am so late. The tracks are very bad. But I did the journey in three days." His manner struck me as slightly unusual, but then I knew he was an opium-smoker. "If I had known you were coming," I said, joking, "I would have gone out myself and caught Bandoola and had him tied up. Now go and have a hot meal with my servants."

Aung Net emptied the mail-bag and then followed San Pyoo out. The mail was all a man could want: home mail from England, home mail from my wife and, besides official correspondence, a bundle of newspapers which I could read at my leisure. Having read the letters, I went on writing the replies which San Pyoo could take when he left again, dependent on the floods.

Aung Net returned after a short time. I took no notice of him but his presence irritated me while I was writing. He fiddled about at the jungle apology for a dressing-table, a small folding camp-table on which I kept a travelling looking-glass, brushes, comb and so on, together with a photograph of Susan and one of Molly Mia.

"Don't bother now, Aung Net," I said. "I am busy."

He went out but in two minutes he was back again, fidgeting with the mosquito net. He raised it and re-adjusted it in exactly the same position.

"What *is* the matter, Aung Net?"

He knelt down and in Shiko posture with both hands together before his face, he said, "I fear to tell you,

Thakin. But San Pyoo says that Po Lone is poisoning Thakin Ma."

San Pyoo had been afraid to tell me himself, but when Aung Net brought him in, with a blanket round his shoulders and shivering with a malarial ague, he produced from a dirty piece of paper a grubby pill about the size of a Beecham's. "This was given me by Joseph the cook, who found it in Po Lone's pocket," he said. "Joseph says that Po Lone dissolves a pill like this in every drink he takes to Thakin Ma."

I took the pill and said, "And how is Thakin Ma? Is she ill?"

"She was riding a pony the morning I left," San Pyoo answered. "She looked very well."

I sent them both away. The idea that Susan was being poisoned seemed impossible: and yet it was not impossible. Nothing was impossible in Burma. One of my forest assistants was a taxidermist. In his cupboard he kept a bottle of a preservative called Atlas Skin, which three Burmans had stolen and drunk under the impression that it was a sort of wine. They all died of arsenical poisoning. I nibbled the pill. It tasted like dirt but for all I knew it might be arsenic. God knew there was enough of it lying around the camps. It was used in powder form as the main elephant tonic.

The idea seemed impossible. But there was the pill. On such a matter Joseph and San Pyoo would not lie. I looked out at the curtain of rain which hung from the roof of the veranda and cursed the monsoon and the mud of the jungle.

The Singaung was far too ill to help, so I sent for Po Toke, told him the story and asked him what he thought the quickest way would be to get a message through to headquarters.

"I am too old for such a journey," said Po Toke. "But I could take a messenger on Bandoola as far as Pahauk Wa, after which there are no more rivers to cross except the Minya; and for that the messenger could get a canoe."

"But what messenger?" I asked, "San Pyoo is down with fever."

"So he says," Po Toke agreed. "But he is afraid. Saw Pa Soo, the Karen boy who is spearman to Hao Zone the young tusker, is afraid of nothing, night or day. And no matter what hour he arrived, your night watchman, who is also a Karen, would accept a message from him."

I promised that I would reward Po Toke and the Karen boy, if he got through. Then I scribbled a hurried note to Susan warning her to accept no drinks from Po Lone but to prepare everything herself, and saying that I hoped to be back in headquarters in three days, if I could negotiate the floods.

I handed the note to Saw Pa Soo, instructing him to hand it personally to my wife and promising that if he got through in record time I would promote him. It was almost dark when I saw Bandoola ridden by Po Toke cross the river, with the young Karen, almost naked, sitting behind him. I hated to see them go, because I was asking them to do something which I could not do myself in such conditions.

It was dark when Po Toke reported back to me that Saw Pa Soo had gone to the main ridge in order to avoid all creek-crossings. That way, I realised, he ran the greater danger of attack from bear, tiger or bison.

I tried to eat something. I certainly drank something. I had done all I could. But the thought of Susan's danger at headquarters and the Karen boy struggling through the monsoon-sodden jungle in the darkness gave me no rest. I went to bed and tried to sleep. But I kept thinking, "If a Karen can do it, so can you." The noise of the flood-water in the creek seemed to me to be abating. I got up and dressed and called a servant to prepare hot tea. This I laced with whisky, fifty-fifty, and filled two empty bottles with it. Those and a small tin of biscuits should see me through. I asked Aung Net if he would come with me. He agreed and added, "Why not take San Pyoo?"

"But he is sick."

"He is sick with worry, Thakin."

When San Pyoo knew I was going, he jumped at the suggestion. I placed Po Toke in charge of all I left behind: gun, rifle, specie-box and all my camp equipment. The only thing I took with me was my revolver.

Bandoola took us over the creek. The rain had stopped and the water was rapidly falling. We "camp-hopped," going, that is, from the camp in one watershed to that in the next. We reached Tha Zan's at dawn and were revived with some hot rice; then on to Maung Ohn's, who accompanied us to Ba Tun's. On our last lap we were alone.

I lost all fear of wild game. The only shock I had was from our own elephants grazing at large. They became more alarmed at being disturbed at night than any other animals we encountered. Occasionally we heard some wild beast crashing off as if to make way for us in our hurry. It was the only time in all my years of forest life that I attempted night-marching off any beaten tracks. From that day to this I do not know how San Pyoo found his way.

We travelled night and day without a let-up. The third night was the worst. The tea-whisky was finished, the bottles were discarded. I cursed the weight of my revolver and also my torch, except at those moments when it was needed. We were already nearly dead beat when we embarked on five miles of elephant track, which in places was three feet deep in mud. We kept a look-out for Saw Pa Soo's tracks but there was no sign of them. Added to physical exhaustion was the anxiety of what we should find at the other end, the imagination of appalling scenes of tragedy. San Pyoo tried to persuade me that I should find some shelter, while he went on ahead.

We reached the Tunbin Forest rest-house, from which a real forest-road led the remaining four miles to headquarters. On the veranda we both nearly collapsed. The dawn was coming up fast. San Pyoo persuaded me to try to sleep while he went to a village about a mile away in the hope of hiring a pony. I lay back in a chair and as I closed my eyes I felt sleep come beating over me in waves. I fought against it feebly because I was afraid that if I once went off, I should not wake up for a very long time.

Suddenly I became conscious of the beat of galloping hoofs. I opened my eyes and there around the bend of the forest road came Susan, mounted on Nicky, and followed by my Syce on Little Me.

I got to my feet and shouted to them, waving till I saw that they had noticed and were cantering over. There was no need to ask Susan how she was. She was blooming with health. The agony of the last two and a half days had been nothing but a nightmare.

I left San Pyoo, who had friends in Tunbin. My Syce walked home, while I rode Little Me. Saw Pa Soo, so Susan told me, had arrived at headquarters in the early hours of the previous night. Susan had been wakened by the Karen night-watchman staring through the mosquito net and telling her to come quickly. She read the note and scribbled at the bottom, "Don't worry. Have gone on the waggon. Am fit as can be."

And yet there remained the mystery of the pills. I was too exhausted to bother about it at the moment. I went straight to bed and slept till noon. By evening I had fever.

We never discovered for certain what Po Lone was trying to do. The police theory was that, knowing what had happened to the other servants, he was afraid— with some justification—that he would be dismissed, and that while he was on leave he obtained from the priest in his village these pills which would have the magical effect of winning him Susan's favour. If that was so, he was mistaken. He got the sack at once.

I sent orders for Po Toke to move my camp to head- quarters. As happened so often after a tour of the jungle in the monsoon, I was in for a bad spell of malaria. I promoted Po Toke back to the position of Singaung in charge of the camp and promised him that if I could help it he would never lose charge of Bandoola.

Saw Pa Soo on receiving his reward asked for leave to go to Karenni and I never saw him again. San Pyoo continued for some years with his work as jungle messenger, which he combined with a remunerative traffic in opium to the camps. In the end the drug by which he made his best living caused his death. He ran out of opium when he was in the jungle. He had come to rely on it utterly, and in his attempt to reach the main river and renew his supplies before he collapsed, he was drowned trying to shoot the Myittha rapids on an empty kerosine oil-drum, a quicker and less painful death, the Burmans said, than if he had died from want of his drug.

CHAPTER THIRTEEN

CONTENTMENT IN COMPANY

Not very long after my marriage I was transferred from the North Western to the North Eastern forests of Burma. I use the word "transfer" but I mean none of the comfortable things associated with that word. There was no question of getting on to a launch or a train and arriving at the new headquarters in a matter of a few days. We walked every foot of the way and the journey took five months, because my instructions were to inspect other large Forest Areas *en route* and to cope with certain problems which were known to have arisen.

As it was the open season, I took Susan with me. I must confess that I was slightly apprehensive. I was not thinking of the strain of those armed parties during the rebellion, for then we had been pitchforked together for self-protection. I was thinking rather of journeys which had begun with men I regarded as friends and which had ended in coolness, if nothing worse; and of one particular marriage begun in happiness which had ended by husband and wife crowning one another with the wedding presents.

The manufacturers of camp equipment have never apparently turned their designers on to the problems of matrimony under canvas. As far as I know, no one, not even Kayem himself, ever invented a double camp-bed. One night Susan complained that there seemed to be a peculiar and rather offensive smell in her bed. When I stripped it the next morning, I saw that the leather thong which tautened the canvas had been smeared with a rank-smelling grease—fat from a roasted wild pig, as I found out later. I asked my servant what the hell he had been up to; and he grinned and said, "It stops it creaking." And that was as near as we got to special camp equipment for a honeymoon couple.

But there was no need for me to be frightened. Susan for one thing was not new to the jungle. She had often toured with her uncle, who spent every moment which he could spare from conserving forests stalking and shooting big game. Camp life to her was a familiar and enjoyable thing as a young girl. But the sort of life which I had to lead added something to her experience which she had not found with the great hunter and fisherman. She came to enjoy all the living things of the jungle: the birds, the beasts and the flowers. She treated the jungle as another woman might treat her garden, the more delightful because it was full of surprises. She would collect as many as twenty different species of wild flowers on the march, likening them to those of the Cornish hedgerows.

I had previously enjoyed my loneliness in the jungle, despite all the longings for companionship which at times assailed me. I enjoyed it because it brought me private joys which I could not believe that anyone would ever share with me. The discovery that Susan could not only share my pleasures but also enlarge them was the perfection of my happiness.

The first place where we camped for any time was in a valley which we reached after ten marches. It was another case of timber stranded on its way down-river. In this case the trouble was not the obstruction of boulders or the anger of the Nats. It was purely and simply that a river had changed its course. Over the wide, desolate valley in a sea of elephant grass four square miles in area were scattered logs of all shapes and sizes, like bodies on an overgrown battlefield.

My heart sank when I first saw the scene. The mud was knee-deep. There were a few large cotton trees which could serve as landmarks, it was true. But there was such a labyrinth of old channels and new channels winding their way through the grass that it took me a month even to plot the chaos. (To-day a reconnaissance aircraft could do the job more accurately in the same number of minutes as it took me days.)

I couldn't attempt to count the stranded timber. Being cautious I estimated it as a mere ten thousand. Ten thousand logs, some half-submerged in mud, some lying in backwaters or pools of stagnant water; others in heaps of twenty or thirty entangled with all the debris brought down by the last monsoon floods. It was at any rate a change from the dense jungles. We were at least encamped under an open sky and warmed during the day by the tropical November sun.

Most of the scattered logs were a couple of miles from the main channel of the river. To get them to the channel was a herculean task, yet unless it was done before the next monsoon half these precious logs would sink into the mud and disappear for all time. When I contemplated my rough survey map, I realised that a herd of a hundred elephants would not be enough to drag every log to the channel. I doubted even if elephants could reach half the logs, because of the soft mud and the silt. I decided that the best thing would be to cut lanes through the dense elephant grass, joining the main piles of timber. These lanes would be deepened by the elephants dragging as many logs as they could to the main channel, and when the monsoons came I should have to trust that the new floods would follow these channels.

I started with forty heavy elephants, mostly tuskers. One of the first camps I called up was Po Toke's and, remembering his performance in the Wabobin Gorge,

I stipulated Bandoola by name. From the main riverine villages I contracted for a hundred pairs of timber-
dragging buffaloes to supplement the elephants. From
the same villages I brought in Burman coolies to cut and
hack the lanes through the elephant grass.

This wild desolate valley soon became alive. Within
a couple of days of their arrival the coolies, the buffalo-
men and the oozies had mastered the geography of an
area which had taken me a month to map. The whole
tract which at first had appeared featureless soon became familiar. Like the trenches in the 1914–18
war, junctions of channels, cuttings, timber-stacks and
pools of water were all named within a few days, named
by their shapes or after incidents which had happened
there. It made me realise how comforting is man's
gift for place-names.

I put a young Anglo-Burman in charge of the work
and from time to time he came to see me to discuss his
problems and receive instructions. His camp was at
the edge of the forest on the main channel, about a mile
away from ours. One evening he reported that Po Toke
was not pulling his weight with Bandoola, or Bandoola
with Po Toke. The next day I went to Po Toke's
section to see for myself. My impression was that the
oozie whom Po Toke had put to ride Bandoola did not
know how to handle him. I suggested that Po Toke
should ride Bandoola himself. It was then that Po Toke
reminded me of Bandoola's experience of being bogged

down in the mud as a calf, which I related earlier. It had happened over thirty years before. Bandoola was massive. He was full grown. He was the prime elephant of the Burmese forests. But he was shy of mud.

Po Toke might not be reliable in the case of killer elephants with abscesses, or when a rebellion was brewing, or when he was taking to himself a second wife. But I did not distrust him now. Very few men or women reach maturity without some scars of childhood, some secret fear or weakness. If that was true of humans, why should it be different with animals?

I had spoken often to Susan about Bandoola, and now I had the chance to show him to her, the elephant in whose training I had had the pride to share, the most magnificent of the beasts with whom I had worked.

We had five dogs in that camp, each as different in character as five children and each, alas! because the life of a dog in the jungle is even shorter than elsewhere, to be a source of grief in its departure.

There was the bull-terrier Sally, whom I rescued from her owner, a bull-terrier fancier and judge. He wanted to put her down because she had a growth in the womb which prevented her having any more puppies. One might have thought that a growth in the womb would produce an abstinent state of mind. But not in

Sally. She was permanently on heat and the most promiscuous animal I've ever known.

But in that camp she found a pastime even more exciting: otter-hunting by moonlight. The large pools left from the floods and the changed course of the river teemed with fish, in which schools of otters were having the feast of their lives. The muddy sandbanks were bee-hived with their holes, and when we were standing by a pool, it was common enough for a dog otter to surface and bark, as if to say, "Clear out. I was here first."

Sally wouldn't think of clearing out. She worried their lives out day and night. If we had been in the jungle instead of this wide, open valley, she would have been picked off by a panther the first night. As it was, she could let herself go in a frenzy of hunting. She never caught an otter but she drove them from pool to pool. Nothing we could do would stop her.

She was snow-white with pink eyes and she protected the other four dogs as if they were her puppies. When we passed through a village and the village dogs came out to yap and bark at ours, Sally brought up the rear as if daring them to attack.

Age caught up with her at last, age and the cursed hook-worm. We cured her several times, we thought, but back they came to sap every good drop of blood. She grew so weak that one night I thought she would die in her sleep. But in the early morning I woke up and through my mosquito net I saw her cross the floor of my bamboo hut like a white ghost towards a rat scratching in the corner. Her tail was as stiff as a poker. She took six paces and then she collapsed. At eight a.m. she was still alive, but I knew that she would never again smack her tail on the floor to me.

I had taken Sally when her owner wanted to destroy her, and now that her natural time had come I felt that I could not destroy her myself. Without telling Susan, I asked the young Anglo-Burman to take Sally down the river in a dug-out canoe, while I took Susan for a walk up the river. "When you get to such and such a place," I said, mentioning a reach a long way down, "put her to sleep after blindfolding her first, then capsize the boat—I've already weighted her—and come back along the bank, like a good fellow."

Susan and I took our walk. We went a long way. But the noise of two shots reached us, echoing up the valley. "What's that?" Susan asked, and when I told her, that was the end of our walk.

There was Bilu, a Chinese chow which was a black ball of fluff I had bartered from some Chinese mule-teers. Every year during the cold season these mule-teers came from Yunnan to do contract work for the large timber firms, transporting rice by mules from the riverine villages to the jungle stores. They always brought several of these attractive dogs to protect their mules in camp. I tried to get them to sell me a bitch or a bitch puppy, but without success. Indeed I only got

Bilu by trading for him a drum of Stockholm tar which they needed for the treatment of their mules' pack-saddle galls.

Bilu had the most amazingly small paws, even for a chow. His ability for learning tricks was remarkable. My wife had only to show him the trick once and he could do it. I often thought a little fortune could be made training these dogs for the circus ring. He had one habit of which we could not break him. He loved to yap at monkeys. He had only to see them in a tree and there he'd sit, yapping away like mad for hours. We would call and call, but he wouldn't take any notice. So we would leave him and hours later, when we had got miles and miles ahead, up he would turn, his little black round tongue hanging seven or eight inches out of his mouth. He felt the heat more than any other dog I possessed. He came of a breed accustomed to the far-distant mountainous regions of China. He was prone to pneumonia, like all dogs which only sleep where it is damp and cool. We pulled him through his first two attacks with a mixture of honey and whisky, half and half. But the third attack was too much for him.

There was Rhona, a golden cocker, a grand true loyal character. She carried a full-sized cock pheasant as easily as a Labrador. A strong runner of a cock jungle fowl was heaven on earth to her. She never failed to find. Susan handled her for me when I was shooting, and how jealous Rhona was of another gun! If in a line of three or four guns she saw a neighbour's dog pick up a bird which I had shot, she needed only half a chance to poach one back on the following beat.

And finally there was Molly Mia, whom Susan had adopted, or rather who had adopted Susan, when I went off to the Andamans. I brought her out from England with a mate, Karl. He, however, lasted only a few months. Chasing a pariah dog, he caught his neck on an iron stake and severed his jugular vein.

Molly Mia was the most intelligent dog I have ever had. It was dangerous to teach her too much. In her early days I persuaded one of my servants to play a game with us. He was to try and touch my keys. Every time he did so, I grabbed them, saying No! sharply. By evening Molly Mia seized whoever tried to touch my keys by the arm, the leg or the buttock. As a game we gave it up. It had become too rough.

I had been slightly jealous at the way Molly Mia transferred her affection to Susan when I left for the Andamans. But when we got married, she shared us, as children share their parents. She was fearless of forest and stream and all that lived therein. At night she would adjust her own mosquito net, which was the shape of a bell tent and slit at one side, and actually tucked herself in. Then she would snap at every mosquito which was inside, after which she would sit on her haunches and look about to see whether anything else remained which might disturb her; and finally she would roll into a ball and sleep.

Like all dogs she loved to retrieve a stick flung into a river, but best of all if it was from a ten- or twelve-foot bank, so that she could leap off into mid-air and land belly-flat with a resounding splash. One evening when I'd flung a stick for her and she was paddle-swimming towards it, I saw with alarm a large water-snake coming down-river, head well above water like a cobra. I called to her, pointing in warning. Molly turned and and with one snap gripped it just behind the head and neck and swam ashore. She never let it go, though it was lashing out like a whip; she just trotted over and dropped it at my feet with a broken neck.

In forest areas where I knew there were no panther, I would intentionally leave something behind in camp, and then when I was ten miles out send her back to fetch it. She enjoyed it as much as a child fetching something for the first time in its life.

On the occasions when to my reluctance I had to leave her behind in camp I did not chain her. She would remain at my command, though she made no effort to hide the fact that she felt hurt.

A curious thing arose out of this. When I left her in camp, she was never far from my thoughts; and this was not because there weren't plenty of other things to occupy my mind in connection with my work. Indeed it was only when this work was difficult and dangerous that I left Molly behind: when for example I was exploring for elephant-dragging paths to by-pass waterfalls or blasting huge boulders with dynamite. On such work one's mind does not have much opportunity to wander, and yet the image of Molly Mia kept obtruding itself on me. It wasn't just an idle picture of the dog, asleep or bored or just waiting for me to return; it was a clear and distinct image of Molly Mia sitting on her haunches, watching for me, listening either for the sound of my voice or some noise in the jungle, a sign that I had come back. There seemed to me to be some curious mental affinity between us.

I then discovered, quite separately, that I was able to make her obey me without my looking at her or speaking. It happened one evening without my realising that I had done it. She was shaking the bamboo floor of the jungle hut and I thought, "For goodness sake, lie down," and she lay down. It was something so unconscious that I couldn't be sure that I hadn't thought aloud. I tried my first experiment. I went on with my work, but I willed Molly Mia to come to my side, and she immediately got up and came to my side.

I then began to will her from longer distances. I started about a hundred yards from camp, out of sight, and as far as possible out of scent. It was uncanny, because she came to me as fast as if I'd called her and she knew already where I was.

The camp where I made this first discovery was be-

side a river. Having tried and succeeded in calling her
from distances as far away as two miles in dense jungle,
I attempted what seemed to me the most arduous of all
experiments. I synchronised my watch and my camp
clock and at six a.m. set off on my forest work, first
crossing the river and later re-crossing it. At noon, when
I was at least four miles away, I withdrew about two
hundred yards away from my Burmans and sat down
and concentrated hard on Molly. Within half an hour
I heard her ranging somewhere near me, and towards
me, sure enough, she came bounding in a minute or two.

The most interesting thing about this was that my
servant Aung Net told me that at noon Molly Mia had
suddenly dashed off exactly as if she had heard me
call; *but she did not cross the river.*

It was because of this very strange bond between us
that I had been so surprised at Molly Mia's instant
change of allegiance to Susan. I tried to discover what
hold I still had on the dog, when we were in the river-
valley camp working on the stranded logs.

I left Molly behind in camp with Susan and we
arranged certain hours when she should watch for re-
actions. We had no expectation that she would come to
me, firstly because I had discontinued the practice of
calling for a long time, and secondly because Susan had
sufficient control over her to prevent it. Yet at each of
the set times Molly suddenly gave that extra prick to her
ears and that look around camp as if she'd heard my

whistle or call; when all that had happened was that I had drawn apart some five miles away and was sitting on a log conjuring her image before my mind.

The life-span of a dog is sadly short and in the jungle shorter still. Some years later I was alone in camp with Molly as my only companion. For the first time I noticed her in a mood. She looked through and beyond me. I tied her up. I had a horrible fear of rabies.

Yet I could not bear to see her tied up, a dog that had never been chained. That evening I let her loose to take her for a walk. In the moment I freed her, I knew that I had no control of her. She might never have seen me before.

At first I thought she would make for the jungle. But having got free, she kept circling the camp like a wild animal who had re-found fear. She hid behind trees. But when I reached them, she was gone. I looked round and there she was, still watching me with staring eyes. She was not so much mad as deranged, physically as strong as ever.

At last I gave up the attempt to control her and began to make my way back to camp. As I did so, I suddenly realised that the whole emphasis of the chase had altered. She was now the pursuer and I the pursued. Any moment I thought she'll really go mad and attack me. My gun was in the tent. Molly Mia was padding behind me. I was not only very frightened but heart-broken.

I am not controlled by superstitions as a rule. Most of the worthwhile things which men have done seem to me to have been accomplished by flying in the teeth of superstition. But at that moment I remembered the Burmese superstition that no mad dog will attack a man on all fours—the argument being presumably that the dog will realise that any man on all fours is even madder than it is. At any rate I went down on all fours and for good measure I snarled; and Molly Mia disappeared.

By the time she came back, I had my gun and I shot her dead. She certainly had rabies. At first all I felt was grief for the dog. But then I realised that though Molly Mia had not bitten me, I might have been infected by her saliva entering a cut or slight abrasion. I knew that I had no chance of getting treatment during the next ten days, the time-limit stated by pundits within which injections were effective. My grief gave way to anxiety, none the less agonising because it might be utterly unfounded. The incubation period for rabies is extraordinarily variable. It may be as short as two weeks and it may even be a matter of years.

The patient's symptoms during the premonitory stage are deep mental depression, restlessness and indefinite fear. These were symptoms I immediately imagined. I also suffered from imagination of thirst and desired violently to drink—though this was a symptom with which I had long been familiar. For weeks and even months the fear would come to me that as I raised the whisky to my lips, I should be seized with a violent suffocative spasm of the muscles of swallowing and breathing, succeeded by a feeling of intense alarm and distress. This, thanks be to God, was a stage which I never reached, but it was years before the apprehension left me.

I enjoyed our five dogs in the camp of the valley of stranded timber more than I have enjoyed any, because there was Susan to share them with me. It was my first chance also to enjoy some other jungle pets. Previously I had had to refuse them, because there was no one responsible in camp to look after them for me. The Burmans themselves, believing in the sanctity of all life, would adopt all sorts of young animals which had lost their parents, even to the extent of their women giving suck to the unweaned mammals.

The first of our many jungle pets in this camp was a baby hog-deer, whom we called Rikki. My men had shot its mother. When they found the baby, they handed it to me, a strange little thing about the size of a soda-water bottle. Its tiny slots were as small as the end of a fountain pen. Its eyes were liquid brown and looked as if they were always about to burst into tears.

When I got back to camp, I set it on the table to surprise Susan. She grabbed it with a scream of delight, while the five dogs, hunters all, squatted on their haunches, hoping it would leap among them.

But very soon the dogs accepted Rikki, and within a week the baby hog-deer made the "sixth dog" on our evening walks. Rikki was the best to heel; he stuck as close to Susan's ankles as if he was at heel to his mother. Rikki learned to answer to a whistle-call as quickly as any dog, springing from some bed of leaves near camp where he had lain up.

Our own dogs made a fuss of Rikki, who came to consider that all dogs were the natural friends of hog-deer. It was his undoing. After we had had him for about a year, he was attacked by a brindled bull terrier belonging to another Assistant and died as a result.

Our next orphans were chicks of the wild jungle fowl. I had long known how to catch these chicks when flushing a hen bird during the early hot-weather nesting season. I used to stand absolutely still for about five minutes after the mother bird flushed and then, kneeling down silently, I tickled the dry leaves with my fingers. It was rather like a conjuring trick, because as soon as they heard the noise eight to twelve tiny little balls of fluff would scuttle in from all round me to take cover under my hand. But I had long since abandoned putting them in my pocket, because I had given up all hope of rearing them.

The valley we were in seemed to be a sort of breeding area and to amuse Susan I took a clutch back with me to camp. They were very like day-old pheasant chicks, but instead of admiring them, Susan immediately took them and popped them under the camp-bed blankets. She reared the whole clutch and many dozens later in this way.

On the march they were even more favoured. Susan would drop them one by one into the depths of her deep-plunge-neckline tunic where they cuddled up. She had found the secret of rearing jungle chicks.

I found that Susan shared with me the envy of the animals for something they have which man has lost, an understanding of their environment so acute that they seem able to foresee what is going to happen. How is it that the barking deer always barks that familiar call of the jungle when the river is going to reach full spate that night? I came to know it as a certain forecast. How did it know so surely? And anyway why should it bark? I asked the jungle Burmans, but none of them had an answer. It was years before I noticed that, following the bark, there would be what seemed like the ghosts of this lovely little animal fleeting across the river-bed and out of sight. It was merely the male calling his harem to the safe side of the bank before the frightening, thunderous flood poured down. I believed in the forecast of the deer so strongly that I often struck camp immediately and crossed to the other bank, if that would suit me better for starting in the morning.

Elephants were not so sensitive to the threat of water, perhaps because they had less to fear. But they certainly reacted quickly enough to the threat of fire. They knew even better than men that forest streams were God's fire-lines, and hearing the crackle of a forest fire they would put a stream between them and it as soon as possible, yet it seemed with no hurry.

When there were tropical storms, elephants would avoid certain forest canopies. Moving to open ground and well away from trees, they would stand without a movement of ears, trunk or tail, their eyes half-closed, waiting for the flash of lightning descending the green tree and then for the crack of thunder, their bodies drawn up in tension.

Once on a very close day I arrived ahead of my elephants at an old forest rest house which was very dilapidated and had seldom been used for the last twenty years. I couldn't make up my mind whether to use it for the night or to pitch my tent nearby. I was enjoying the stillness and eeriness of a place which, once cleared, had almost reverted to nature, when suddenly there was a terrific snort and a stampede of hooves from the back of the rest house. I had disturbed a full-grown bull bison in the tall grass inside the compound fence. He went at full gallop straight at the four-foot three-bar teak fence. He was a magnificent creature, quite seventeen hands at the withers. With his short, stocky legs tucked under him he took the fence like a perfect hunter, but riderless, and the natural oil oozing from his broad back shone like brilliantine.

"A strange place to find a bison," said my gun-boy follower, and he added it was "Ike Thee," a Burmese expression used to describe the atmosphere which has no English equivalent, because in England there is never the sort of solid jungle stuffiness which seems to need a filter before you can breathe.

I sat and tried to enjoy a pipe. Shortly afterwards the elephants arrived, chirping with joy at the prospect of being unloaded. They were halted, as was usual, outside the compound while they relieved themselves, and then brought up to the veranda which had been built as high as an elephant's back to make unloading easy.

The pack saddlery was removed and arranged in line along the rails of the fence over which the bison had jumped. Heavy jungle grew up to within fifty yards of this fence, and the animals as they were released entered it, feeding at their will. As they went I looked them over to see their condition and then I settled in and had a meal myself. It was stifling hot, but I saw to my surprise that the six elephants had returned from the jungle; and not only that, they had completely left the shade. They were standing right out in the open under the blazing sun in what appeared to be the hottest spot they could have chosen. They were all standing perfectly still, as if lost in thought. I had never seen elephants look quite like that before and I wondered why.

But it was so hot I did not care. There had been a

wind like the blast from an open furnace door scuffling
the dry bamboo leaves. Then the wind dropped and
the temperature rose still higher. There was a terrible
silence. Not a leaf moved.

I stood up as a most peculiar sensation came over me
—as if I was not wholly land-borne and yet not wholly
air-borne. From very far away—perhaps from India
it seemed or from Tibet—came a low rumbling. I
strained my ears, trying to think what it could be, when
suddenly the whole forest swayed its topmost canopy
before my eyes and then the tree boles creaked and
groaned. The six elephants swayed in time with each
other and the old forest rest house swayed with them,
creaking on its rough-hewn tree-trunk posts. And I
swayed too, in the opposite direction, like a sailor on a
boat coming into a swell.

Then the earth shook like a wet spaniel shaking its
coat. Millions of leaves and old dead branches showered
to the ground, but there was no resounding crash. The
trees and more importantly the rest house were still
standing. The Burmese belief is that the world is
carried on the shoulders of four elephantine creatures,
and when one of the monsters wants to change shoulders,
the earth quakes. I ran down the steps just in case one of
the other three should feel the same way about it.

But it was over. The stillness that succeeded the
quake was broken by the shouting of my camp men.
The elephants, as though they had finished attending

some solemn ceremony, left the clearing and re-entered the jungle to make up for lost time. "It won't come back," said my gun-boy; "*they* know."

I found that Susan, though interested in these stories about animal instinct and the habits of elephants, had a streak of scepticism in her. Like Thomas Dydimus, she wanted to see for herself. One night she woke me to listen to the sounds of what she imagined to be a terrific elephant-fight going on down-river.

At first there was the deep low rumbling-dumbling-mumbling of several elephants engaged in conversation. It was rather like a line of racing cars tuning up their powerful engines. Then there was a terrific shrill trumpet, as if one had stripped its gears. Then silence for about ten minutes. Then the whole thing started all over again.

"Don't you worry," I said; "it's only a herd of wild elephants." We got up and together we built up the large log fire which had died down since we had retired to bed. As it began to flare up, I said, "Perhaps it's Toomai of the Elephants." "The elephant dance?" she said, "but you told me you didn't believe in that." "If those elephants don't move on," I said, "I'll guarantee that in three days' time I'll show you one of Kipling's so-called dance-floors. And maybe we can prove it really is a maternity ward after all."

I had already found two of these dance-halls, but I

had never managed to find any physical proof of my conviction that they were maternity wards. But then I had never been in at the birth or first dance like this. And though we were some distance from the herd, we could hear everything that was going on next door almost as clearly as if we were living in a modern block of luxury sound-proof flatlets.

For three nights and three days the earnest mumbling and the strident trumpeting went on, the intervals growing longer on the last day. It became our sole topic of conversation. Had it been born yet? Is it a girl or a boy? How will it ever keep up with the other elephants when they move on? Can the mother really pick it up and carry it for the first three days if disturbed?

On the fourth morning at dawn I watched Susan wake up. She stretched her arms and yawned; and then she said, "I didn't hear Toomai's pals last night."

"Now we can go and look," I said.

At first she was disappointed by what she saw, just a clearing where the ten-feet-tall elephant grass had been trodden down, with a lot of droppings on the outer edges and a few inside.

We had with us one gun-boy, Po See, to whom I explained as we stopped on the edge of the clearing that there were only two things I was looking for, the footprint of a baby elephant or any signs of an afterbirth. Taking no chances of our footprints spreading confusion,

I sent Po See into the main ring to trek any sign of a calf's footprint. He was a boy of the jungle but he claimed no knowledge. I grew impatient watching him —impatient with disappointment, for though he bent down studying the ground, he could give no clue. At last I called out, "Do you know what you are seeking, or have you forgotten like a child what I told you?"

At that he stood up and, looking at me with an expression of forbearance, he said, "There is no sign of the baby's footprints because the large feet of the older elephants obliterate them, and there is no sign of the afterbirth because the mother eats it so that there will be no trace left to whet the tiger's appetite."

This retort was pretty crushing in its quiet way and I was glad that Susan's Burmese wasn't very good. I told her that the reason why the mother ate the afterbirth wasn't purely to cover the tracks. Veterinary research seems to show that the afterbirth contains a hormone which stimulates milk-production, though others believe it has a cleansing action.

Susan and I joined in the search, but we were no more successful. We followed the tracks of the herd across the creek, but there wasn't a sign of a baby elephant's prints, even on the long sand-spit from where the herd had entered the jungle and passed on. We returned to the clearing. It was most dispiriting and I sensed that Susan's scepticism was getting the upper hand, that I might be forced back on pointing out that

Po See took for granted what I was trying to prove. But suddenly Susan said, "Send Po See back to camp to get Rhona. If there was even a stain, Rhona could find it."

It had been one of our marriage-pacts that while I shot over my gun-dogs, Susan was to work and train them. (I did not think much of women shooting.) So when Po See brought Rhona, he and I sat down to watch, while Susan and the dog worked the ground. It was rather hard on the little cocker, because she had no idea of what she was looking for. But her tail and stern wagged back and forth as if to say, "Don't worry. I'll find it, whatever it is."

Then suddenly she stopped dead, turned on her back and rolled and rolled in the earth and dust. I jumped up. She was defleaing herself by rolling on the putrid ground. "Don't scold her," I said, "she's found something." And, sure enough, trampled in the ground beneath her was a small portion of putrid afterbirth. Over it we placed small boulders from the creek and returned to camp, satisfied that not many miles away a baby elephant was enjoying its first few miles of the march of life in company with its mother and relations. We in our devious Western way had proved something which to Po See was so self-evident that it needed no proof.

MATTERS OF LIFE AND DEATH

THE last time that I saw Bandoola before I left the northern forests, he was dying; dying, what is more, from the most inglorious of complaints, colic brought on by over-eating.

I received a message from Po Toke urging me to come quickly, because Bandoola was "down." When a sick elephant goes down, it's the worst of signs. It means that he has given up hope of ever standing up again.

Luckily it was noon when I got the message. Bandoola was down half a mile from Po Toke's camp and I reached him in time to work on him in daylight. When I asked Po Toke what was wrong with Bandoola, he professed that he had no idea. But one look at the elephant was enough. His belly was distended to bursting point. He lay on his side, his eyes staring and his trunk spread out in front of him like some prehistoric reptile.

When I taxed him, Po Toke confessed that when tethered in camp the night before Bandoola had got at the paddy in the rice go-down. With his trunk he had broken off the bamboo matting wall chip by chip until he had made a hole large enough for his tusk to puncture the rice bags. Then, inserting his trunk, he siphoned it out by his trunk, surely and silently all night long. Next morning his oozie noticed the damage to the go-down; but all he thought of was the robbery of the precious rice and the row which he himself might get into if it was found out. If he kept quiet, he thought, he might not be discovered.

Within an hour Bandoola went to drink. The gases created by the mixture of water and paddy blew him out and in agony he had collapsed.

We all agreed that unless we could get him up, he would die. But the question remained, how should we get him up? Twisting an elephant's tail won't shift him. Po Toke had already tried putting green chili-juice, the Burmese counter-irritant, into Bandoola's eyes. It had inflamed them but had made no difference to the elephant's position.

How, I asked myself, can one make an elephant belch? or vomit? or break wind? The belly was visibly distending before my eyes, like a balloon being steadily inflated before an ascent. Not that there was any pros-pect of Bandoola becoming air-borne, the frame was too massive, the gases not volatile enough. The fear was that he would explode, a sort of elephantine time-bomb. If Bandoola had been a Burman suffering from stricture, I could have stuck a knife or a sharpened smoked bamboo in the exact spot to relieve the trouble. But where you punctured an elephant to relieve him of superfluous gases was as much a mystery to me then as it still is.

"Send for Poo Zone and Swai Zike with dragging gear," I ordered. "If we don't get him up, he'll be dead in half an hour." Po Toke's long oily hair was down his back, and when I spoke of Bandoola dying, he was terrified. He set off for Poo Zone and Swai Zike, who were working near the camp, while we who stayed behind worked hard to keep Bandoola's thoughts down to earth and prevent his spirit wandering to another plane of existence, either higher or lower in the Buddhist scale. We whacked him with bamboos; we soused him with water from the creek; we beat him on the most sensitive of his public parts, his toe-nails. But would he budge for us? No! he was literally blowed if he would.

I had heard tales of two African elephants supporting a wounded comrade either side to help it to escape, though no Indian shikar tale has dared as much. My idea, when the two tuskers arrived, was to use them to lift Bandoola up. But it was a hopeless failure. Both animals head to head with their tusks below the barrel of Bandoola's back could only move him a foot or so. There wasn't a hope of lifting him up.

In desperation I decided to roll him over. He was down on his off side. So we attached Poo Zone's dragging-chains to Bandoola's underneath off fore-leg and Swai Zike's to the underneath off hind-leg. Together the two tuskers took the strain, dragging breast to breast, so even and so gentle in their combined action that I felt sure they understood the delicacy of the action.

Bandoola's legs gradually rose until they were pointing to the sky. But his head remained where it was and for a moment I was afraid that it would break his neck as the body twisted. Then there was a sudden struggle as Bandoola's huge head turned under the exertion of his own strength. He groaned—it was the first sound I had heard from him—and agonising though it was as a sound, to hear any sound was encouraging. For a moment his trunk waved in the air. His mouth opened, gulping. Then the whole body rolled over and fell with a terrific thud on the near side. It was rather like turning a very heavy feather mattress, and I was afraid that he was going to be as limp and inanimate on the near side as he had been on the off. But something was shifted. He seemed to deflate on one side and then he struggled to his feet. He was up.

We hurriedly unleashed Poo Zone and Swai Zike, and placed one on each side of him, like two friends trying to support a drunk between them while the policeman passes.

The effort of getting him up had forced some stringy undigested bamboo from his lower bowel. It hung from him in strands. I emptied it as far as I could, plunging in my arm a dozen times as far as the armpit.

The two men holding the tail aside were suddenly overpowered by a swish of it. They lost grip. For an agonising moment, my arm, which was buried to the shoulder, was under strain of snapping. I couldn't pull my arm out because of the pressure of the elephant's flanks and this confounded tail battered at my head.

This was in fact the first sign of recovery. The oozies caught his tail-brush. I drew out my hand and arm. And my job of elephantine plumbing was over. The stoppage was unblocked and nature relieved him of his inflated gas as if he had been punctured.

I gave orders for him to be secured and starved for twenty-four hours and then hand-fed. Within the day he had recovered.

Knowing that I shouldn't see Po Toke again for some years—if ever, because he was an ageing man—I had him up to say good-bye. I had learned so much from him about elephants and jungle that I owed him a debt of gratitude; and he had taught me also quite a lot about the limitations of human trust. I had at first regarded him, even despite Willie's warning, as a man on whom one could rely. Willie's analysis of his character was not right. It was not that he was an outsider to Bom-

bine. Bombine had become his mainstay. Through
Bombine he had accumulated several thousand rupees
in the Provident Fund on which he could rely in his old
age. The flaws were in his own character. Perhaps
from his point of view the desertion during the rebellion was not a flaw, but the act of a Burmese patriot. We
never discussed it because officially he had overstayed
his leave and that was all. His ruling passion had become Bandoola. Though there had been a time when
he had neglected Bandoola because of the second wife
he had taken, that was all over. There had been no
children in this case either and the girl went back to her
village. Po Toke's adventures with women were
ended. Perhaps he realised that the cause of Ma Pyoo's
barrenness lay not in her but in him. In the same way,
his career as an elephant trainer was over. With age he
had shrivelled up and grown smaller. He was an
average headman, no better and no worse than a
hundred others. But he still remained the man who
understood Bandoola better than any other man in the
jungle.

Now that he was old, the other oozies called him
"U" Po Toke, not "Maung" Po Toke. But I knew that
he would never reach that position of respect in which
he was addressed as "Sayah," the learned, learned
though he was about Bandoola.

He had long since risen to the position in which he
wore the white coat of authority. In Ma Pyoo's day it

had always been starched with rice and spotlessly clean. Now it was creased and off-white.

His hair had turned grey, and although it was long, it was untidily knotted. His hands however were very clean and he took pains to draw my attention to the nail on the little finger of his left hand which he had grown to a length of at least half an inch, in a pathetic attempt to show himself a man of authority. He had also tried to grow a beard. It consisted of two hairs, which tried to make up in length what they lacked in number. As he spoke, he continuously stroked and played with them.

These little attempts to impress were really quite unnecessary, because the old man was still handsome. His Kadu or Shan blood had given him a fair skin. His nose was far more chiselled than the normal Burman-Mongolian features. To see him smile was always a pleasure. He had a beautiful set of even white teeth, which he had not stained by the loathsome habit of chewing betel nut. He maintained that it was only the rice-eating races that had good teeth or could make good hunters. Beef-eaters, he said, gave off a scent so strong that even domesticated buffalo could pick it up a mile away.

We sat outside my tent as the evening sun dropped behind the western hills. The nearby ranges were cut in silhouette against the sky. There might have been no forests on their precipitous slopes for all they showed in the deep shadow. Po Toke pointed to one escarpment they called Lovers' Leap, the tree line of which showed against the orange sky like the finest lace, and he remarked that the ghost of the princess who committed suicide there was showing the embroidery of her bodice. "No Ane" was a good description of the oddly shaped hill, for it was like a girl's breast, rising on one side a sheer cliff to four hundred feet and on the other sloping back into the jungle at an angle of forty-five degrees.

Po Toke said that it was a story current with the oozies that a princess eloped with a Burman commoner and because she was not allowed to marry him, they took refuge on the top of the peak; and when they had finished all their food, they finished all their love as well and jumped over the precipice.

He laughed. "That's only an oozie's story," he said, "but they don't laugh at the story of Bo Gyi the old wild tusker and Ma Gyi the old wild female, because that story is true." He hesitated, but I gave him no encouragement to go on. There is no surer way of not hearing a Burman elephant story than to show interest in it. But finding that I didn't press him to continue, Po Toke resumed his narrative. "Bo Gyi and Ma Gyi," he said, "had been spoken of as inseparable companions all their lives and they did not live with a herd. Bo Gyi was a tusker of tuskers and he lived in this part for hundreds of years. And always with him went his mate, Ma Gyi.

"Their names were a legend. When our fathers and our forefathers came upon the footprints of Bo Gyi or

Ma Gyi or on even rarer occasions actually saw them in the flesh, they pronounced the names of these great elephants with deep respect. For these two elephants, wild though they were, molested no one. They damaged no crops.

"Bo Gyi, being a lusty tusker, no doubt begot calves on other females also, but Ma Gyi's calves were all by Bo Gyi. She had no less than nine by him, it was said, and once she was seen with two calves at heel of different ages."

"That's impossible," I said.

"It's not impossible," said Po Toke. "If she had her first calf at the age of twenty-two, with a normal lactation of five years and a gestation of two years, that is with a calf every seven years, her age would be only eighty-five. Those two, Bo Gyi and Ma Gyi, became almost legendary figures, as the happy old couple of the Nankamoo drainage, living together under the shadow of Lovers' Leap."

"Perhaps," I said, joking, "perhaps Bandoola was one of their descendants."

"It may very well be," Po Toke answered, and he looked towards the fading silhouette of Lovers' Leap. "But here is the fantastic part of the story of the great love of these aged elephants. One evening some hunters were camped just where we are now. It was an earlier hour than this. They had cooked their rice and were having their evening meal squatting in a circle, when an oozie said that he had found that evening the carcase of an old elephant, dead and already beginning to stink. But nearby there was an old tusker grumbling and mumbling as if his heart was broken.

"'If that's Ma Gyi,' said one of the others, 'mark my words, Bo Gyi won't last much longer.'

"They went on eating. All hands were busy raising rice to mouths from the wild plantain leaves, when suddenly an elephant trumpeted. Their hands checked as they looked up, and there on the slope of Lovers' Leap they saw silhouetted a huge tusker climbing towards the peak.

"It was Bo Gyi. The hunters stopped eating and watched enthralled. The aged elephant moved very slowly. Often he halted. But he did not feed. He just stood still with his head lowered. Then he moved on again, following the path which had been trodden by the Princess and her lover. It must have taken him an hour to reach the top; and when he got there he stood on the peak looking over the dense forest spread out before him four hundred feet below. He was clearly silhouetted and he seemed to revive himself, because he lifted his head high."

I could see the whole thing, because Po Toke was acting it for me. His arm, as he told of Bo Gyi lifting his head, lifted like an elephant's trunk.

"The hunters were down here watching him, Thakin. And old Bo Gyi surveyed all below him, trunk in the air.

Then suddenly he blew a terrific trumpet, his Last Post. And then slowly, this is what he did." Po Toke opened his mouth wide and with his arm still imitating the trunk he put his tapered fingers like the end of the trunk into his mouth. "He blew his brains out and toppled over the precipice over which the Princess had preceded him, full of love and empty of food."

When I came to reflect on it, I laughed more and more, thinking of the way in which Po Toke had built up my credulity. He was an artist. But at the same time I was glad that I was leaving his forest, because after that performance I could never believe in him again even to the extent which I had before. He had made me laugh for a moment, but at the expense of distrusting him from then on, not consciously perhaps, but deep down. I wished in a way I could have taken Bandoola with me.

CHAPTER FIFTEEN

THE END OF SERVICE

I DID not see Po Toke or Bandoola again for seven years; and then it was under circumstances which were to test all three of us. Po Toke, Bandoola and I had been curiously held together by our service to Bombine. We had worked together comparatively peaceably—in peace-time. But that Po Toke had other loyalties had been shown during the rebellion. And in April 1942, with the Japanese flooding into Burma and the British, civilian and soldier alike, getting out just as fast as they could, I wondered what Po Toke's feelings would be towards the Japanese talk of co-prosperity spheres and the liberation of the oriental peoples.

I saw Po Toke during the retreat. He was still a headman and his elephants, including Bandoola, were bridge-building. Streams of men, women and children, weary and heartbroken, glanced towards the animals as they worked. Buffalo-carts lumbered by, with wheels creaking to ward off the Nats. These were things to which Bandoola was accustomed. But when a strange-looking lorry passed near him with gears grinding, engine roaring, he tried to bolt for his life, or on occasion took up an attitude as if he was going to charge it as some monstrous Nat threatening his peace and ours.

A whole squadron of tanks was routed to cross by our bridges. Po Toke was superb. He talked to Bandoola, pacified him and kept him hard at work, handling the most massive tree-lengths, forty to fifty feet in length. This was the tempo of war, working against time, oblivious of what lay ahead when this job was over. And—once again characteristic of war—when the job was finished, no squadron arrived. One lone, lame tank crossed the bridge. Bandoola watched it from a respectful distance away in the jungle, prepared at any moment to do a bolt.

To those of us who had worked with elephants that retreat was a heartbreaking and humiliating thing. We had to leave behind us the men and animals with whom we had worked for years. The whole structure of Bombine had collapsed—and it must have seemed to Po Toke and hundreds of other oozies, seeing the straggling columns winding towards India, that it had collapsed for ever. I saw Po Toke before I left and I gave him some money. "Hide if you can," I said. "I promise you that I will come back when this Dokha gyi, big trouble, has sorted itself out." I meant it and I tried to make my voice carry the conviction that would outweigh the evidence of what was passing before our eyes.

Po Toke took the money; but he did not look as if he believed what I said. In fact I don't think he believed in anything or anyone any more, except Bandoola. His wives had failed him, or he had failed them. The money which he had expected to receive from the Bombine Provident Fund would never materialise. The British dominion over Burma was being exchanged for a Japanese dominion. I think he felt as old and tired and bitter as he looked.

Bandoola's oozie ran away. And as the rearguard of the retreating army and the last straggling refugees departed towards Assam, Po Toke mounted Bandoola and rode him off. He had loved and tended and coveted this elephant as his own for forty-five years; and now in this moment of defeat Bandoola was his. He rode him by game-tracks known only to himself up and along the ridge of the Teelaung river, and then he dropped into the Kabaw Valley, making for his native village, Witok.

When he reached Witok, he found it in sorry shape. It had been invaded by hordes of evacuees, and the villagers, afraid of cholera and other diseases, had fled into the jungle, knowing that when the rains broke everything moving would be halted and that any unfortunate evacuee overtaken by the monsoons would die in the village.

Po Toke took Bandoola up one of the headwater tributaries of the Witok Creek. He fettered him securely and attached to his fore-fetters two heavy chains twenty feet in length which would prevent the elephant from wandering so far that he could not track him again. Then he went back to his village, or rather to what had been left of it by the evacuees.

The Japanese, who were now in full occupation of Burma, sent out orders that all elephant-riders should report with their animals. The penalty for disobedience was death.

Po Toke went to report. He said that Bandoola, who was a dangerous and savage tusker, had joined the wild elephant herds. No one would ever handle him again. In that case, they said, he could have an appointment mustering as many deserted elephants as he could find. He pleaded that he was old and sick, and he returned to his war-scarred village.

As far as he knew, no one in the village was aware that he had Bandoola hidden. It was not likely that any of them would discover it. Fear and uncertainty had closed down on the country and few people wandered far from their homes. Yet Po Toke lived in dread that some oozie might betray him; or else that one of the Japanese or our own Indian patrols which were beginning to visit the village more frequently would come on Bandoola and shoot him for his ivory. He knew that no strangers would attempt to capture Bandoola any more than they would try to capture a wild tusker.

During the 1942 monsoons Po Toke left the village half a dozen times and returned after five or six days. Each time he found Bandoola, but he knew that every visit was dangerous. His absences made people talk and speculate; the time might come when he would be called on to explain them to the Japanese.

The money which I had given him lasted for six months. His sixth visit to Bandoola he knew would be his last. He would have to find some job with the invaders which would give him food, and Bandoola must be free to fend for himself. He took off the fetters and chains. "Keep clear of wild tuskers and don't fight," he said. "Buddha provided food for you in the jungles. But for me there is nowhere where life is easy. My life is at an end, but I shall not rob you of yours." He patted Bandoola's massive trunk, stroked his smooth tusks and then made his way down-stream towards his unhappy village. Bandoola watched him out of sight and then went back to his eating.

In October there was the usual break in the monsoon, in peace-time a promise to the jungle Burman that the torrential rains would soon be over. But this year the promise turned to a threat. With the end of the rains, the village would be at the mercy of enemy patrols; and for the Burmans, the soldiers of either side were the enemy.

One evening, a few days after his return from his last visit to Bandoola, Po Toke was lying in his hut feeling old, tired and hungry. He had lost all feelings of pride. His few rags of clothes were dirty. His hair hung long and uncombed.

Suddenly he heard a sound which he had not heard for months, the laughter of children, and then a voice which, though it belonged to no one in the village, was familiar. "Yauk byee! Yauk byee!" the children shouted. "He's come! He's come!"

Po Toke peeped through a tiny hole in the matting wall and there standing ankle-deep in mud, he saw Harold Browne with six or seven children scrambling to hold his hands. A young Burmese girl of twenty ran to him and hugged him round his waist, crying with joy.

Old Po Toke for the first time in months hurriedly tied his hair into a bunch and grabbed a piece of cloth and wound it round his head in respect. As he came out of his hut, Harold called to him. "Po Toke, I want to talk to you."

Harold took him on one side and told him that I was at Tamu and I wanted to see him. Harold was more loved by the Burmans than anyone I ever knew. Coming to Witok when all the talk was of how the Japanese were going to sweep on into India, he must have brought heart to them as no one else could. "Of course, I will go to see Williams Thakin Gyi," Po Toke said and he told him how he had kept Bandoola in hiding and that living in the jungle as a hermit was the Anglo-Burman boy of Witok, MacVittie. MacVittie knew that if the invaders caught him, he would be killed. But he had refused to leave his young Burman wife and little girl. Po Toke suggested that MacVittie should come too.

Harold spent that night in the village. I will not say that he slept; all the Burmans seemed to have come to his hut for comfort during the night, old men and women, young women (young men there were none, as they had been taken away as forced labour) and all the children. He gave them money, quinine and, more important than anything, the renewed promise that one day we would return.

When Harold and Po Toke picked up MacVittie at dawn next day, he warned them that an enemy patrol was out, searching for lost elephants in the headwaters of Witok Creek. The news, it seemed to me, made Po Toke slightly crazy. He had hidden Bandoola for so long and now on the very eve of getting him to safety, it appeared as if he was going to lose him after all. He couldn't talk of anything else.

I did not recognise either Po Toke or MacVittie at first. Months of near-starvation had taken a savage toll of their bodies. But it had quickened their spirits. Po Toke had no doubts now where his loyalties lay.

I kept them in camp two days, resting them and feeding them up. Then they set out together to find Bandoola, already looking better physically. Three days later Bandoola was marched back into camp, with both of them riding him. They made an occasion of it, and it was truly an occasion. For this was for all of us the first step in the fight back after that ignominious retreat. Bandoola was presented to me to be enrolled as No. 1 War Elephant, the first of the elephants to fight for the freedom of Burma from the Japanese, and worthy of his glorious name.

What a contrast he was to poor under-nourished old Po Toke! I have never seen even a wild elephant in such magnificent condition. And it was just as well. Three gruelling years of war lay ahead, three years in which those careful considerations of elephant-management which we had built up in peace-time were flung to the winds.

In *Elephant Bill* I told part of Bandoola's war-time story, of the way when evacuating from Assam into India we came to an almost sheer cliff, Bandoola led the elephant train up steps which we cut in the rock and along a narrow path with a precipice on one side. It was a moment of greatness, a heroic moment in which Po Toke had his full share. Without Bandoola and Po Toke we should never have come through. The whole company of us might very well have been lost, the forty-five elephants, the forty armed Karens, the ninety elephant-riders and attendants, the sixty-four refugee women and children and the four officers. I saw there for the first time what I had known for many years, the climax of animal–man relationship.

I will not tell that part of the story again. But there are two other passages in that journey which belong to

Bandoola's story. The first followed closely on his triumph. Coming down from the ridge, we descended into the valley of the Barak river, which was broad and open and swampy.

Once again that childhood experience of Bandoola's asserted itself. He, who had walked beside the precipice, was terrified of swamps. He wouldn't lead. We had to get a young female to lead. But Bandoola would not even follow.

It was infuriating. It looked as if we might have to send Bandoola miles and miles up-river before he could find ground firm enough to follow. Harold Browne and Po Toke went off on a recce and came back reporting that it was possible for Bandoola to make a comparatively small detour to skirt round the swampy ground. And so we all waited a day for this timorous great elephant to catch up with us.

The second passage was when we arrived at last at James Sinclair's tea plantation at the end of our long journey. The only elephant that was still in fine condition was Bandoola. We had not any idea what sort of reception we would meet with when we arrived. It was an occasion for window-dressing, and I put Bandoola at the head of the column. He was a harness elephant if ever there was one; to use him for transport seemed almost an indignity. But on this occasion he strode into the tea-garden, carrying on his back a Siamese "Kah" or pannier, from which protruded the little heads of eight children, all in high fever and some of them delirious. I don't think there was ever an elephant so powerful but with such a fragile cargo.

The last time I saw Bandoola as an individual elephant was five months later when he was marched back to Burma as part of the great offensive. The god of war is a harsh god, who hates individuality more than anything. I myself became impersonal, a machine which was part of a greater machine. The temperament of Bandoola and the temperament of Po Toke, in both of which I had been interested in peace-time, were luxuries which I could not indulge when the war had turned to the offensive. I had to think of elephants and their oozies in tens and then in hundreds and then in thousands. I was part of a new army advancing.

But the elephants weren't and the oozies weren't. *The King's Rules and Regulations* were unknown to them and if they had been known, they would have been even more unintelligible to them than they were to me. The oozies did not obey me because I had a crown and a pip stencilled on an old Bombine khaki shirt. They obeyed me because I was a Bombine man and I knew about elephants. Po Toke left Witok and brought Bandoola with him to work for me. He had no idea that he would become part of the army. In his own mind he was probably still working for Bombine.

I must explain this because it is important, if one is to understand what happened. I am not one of those people who looks back on the war as the happiest years of his life. My life in peace-time had been far too interesting and happy to make such a thing possible. Yet I slipped into the habit of war. I could understand its necessity, even though I was irritated, indeed infuriated, by the orders of General Balls-up relating to elephants.

To Po Toke the whole thing was incomprehensible. We were accredited to the Royal Indian Engineers, and if there was anyone the good Burmese nationalist hated more than a Japanese it was an Indian. Indian engineers knew nothing about elephants. There was continual friction between what the military wanted and what elephants were able to do.

In *Elephant Bill* I told part of the story of Bandoola's end. As the XIVth Army swept back into Burma, Po Toke was put in charge of an elephant camp, feeding two saw-mill units with teak for boat-building. For the facts, let me quote from *Elephant Bill*.

The camp was two miles away from the main military road, and in it one could only just hear the grind of the incessant stream of Army lorries.

Before I went forward to visit Army Headquarters, I told Finch I would visit Po Toke's camp and inspect elephants, for I thought that it would help to keep up the morale of the oozies, who were already becoming impatient for the war to be over, though the elephants had, I think, become completely inured to it.

To my surprise, Bandoola was absent from the parade, and I naturally asked Po Toke where he was.

He replied: "He has been missing for three days, Thakin Gyi."

Whereupon Finch broke in with: "Nonsense! You told me five days ago, when I was last here, that he had not been caught."

I said no more, but, after inspecting the animals, went on into Po Toke's camp, where his men were quartered. I at once sensed that something was wrong, and collected all the elephant-riders and tree-fellers, and spoke to them as follows:

"You all know the difficulties we have with elephants getting lost in peace-time, and how far worse it is in war. Have you all been an organised tracking party, looking for Bandoola?"

No one answered me, so, looking at Po Toke, I asked him: "Have you not organised one?"

Old Po Toke looked pale and worried and replied in a low voice: "There is no trace of his tracks anywhere."

At the risk of incurring the wrath of all the Chief Engineers in Burma, I barked out: "All dragging work here is stopped until Bandoola is found, and there will be no rations in camp either, except plain rice; so get to work at once."

Finch and I went back to camp with the feeling that what we had heard was no normal story of a missing elephant. I went on to Army Headquarters, and Finch arranged to send me a signal when Bandoola was found. But no signal came, and when I got back five days later, I heard that Po Toke had been taken ill, and that the whole camp seemed in a most depressed state, as there was still no trace of Bandoola.

I went straight off, and blasted old Po Toke to hell. The effect was electric. He burst into tears and, blubbering like a school-boy, said to me: "Bandoola is dead within four hundred yards of camp. Go and see him. I am too ill to walk, Thakin Gyi."

Two of the oozies silently led me along a track leading from the camp towards the hills, and before long I could smell the frightful stench of a decomposing elephant. The two oozies stood aside, and I walked on into a cleared patch of short grass. There lay Bandoola, the hero of my march. I could scarcely believe my eyes when I saw him lying dead. But his enormous belly was distended with decomposition—and then I noticed something else was wrong also. His right tusk was gone, and there was only a butt of solid ivory, where it had been sawn off at the lip. The left tusk, half imbedded in mud and earth, on the lower side, had not been taken.

My feelings were a terrible mixture of grief and uncontrollable anger. I was determined to find out the truth. Bandoola was a war casualty. He had been shot. There was a bullet-hole in his forehead, and the bullet must have gone straight through his brain! he had obviously dropped dead where he was standing. As far as I could see, there was no trace of the spot having been visited for several days by any living soul.

I at once put a guard of five Karens, armed with Sten guns, round his carcase, and there was no need to tell them how to act if occasion should arise, or if any intruders came back to get the other tusk during the night. I told them I would be back next morning.

All I could get out of poor old Po Toke was the pitiful statement that Bandoola's oozie had found him dead one evening, ten days before, and on going with the oozie to the spot next morning he had found that the right tusk had been sawn off. In his panic and grief, he had sworn all his men in camp to silence, and had forbidden any of them to go anywhere near the carcase, for fear of the Jungle Nats, which alone would have had the power to kill his unconquerable elephant, Bandoola. He pleaded that he had been unable to face breaking such terrible news, as he knew that my grief and Finch's would be as great as his own. It was useless calling him a bloody fool and cursing him because his prevarication made it far more difficult to discover the culprit. Such arguments meant nothing to Po Toke. Bandoola was dead, and his own interest in life was over. Nothing mattered to him any more. It was late that night before I turned in, and, to put it mildly, I was grieved, angry and perplexed. By noon next day the left tusk had been extracted cleanly from the skull by my Karens, and a .303 bullet extracted from Bandoola's brain. The slenderness of this, my only bit of evidence, can be realised. Thousands of lorries passed nearby along the Army's lines of communication every day. I had inquiries made at every unit in the neighbourhood, but it seemed most unlikely that any sepoy had been guilty, as most of them belonged to non-combatant units. Every check was reported to have been made on ammunition—with the negative results that might have been expected.

There was, however, a Chin village only two miles from the spot. I went there with an armed party, and ordered the headman to produce all firearms within ten minutes. He did so, bringing the owners with their weapons. I disarmed six men, three of whom were armed with old .303-calibre rifles, and put them under close arrest while I made a house-to-house search of their huts, hoping I might find the sawn-off tusk. But I drew a complete blank.

The headman was extremely perturbed when I told him that all the firearms would be confiscated until he either produced the tusk or evidence as to which of his hunters had shot my tusker elephant. Again I drew blank.

I then gave orders to Finch to dismiss Po Toke and Bandoola's oozie, hoping this would produce some reaction by which I could discover the truth. Once more I drew blank.

I do not pretend to have an answer to the mystery of Bandoola's murder. It is a problem which worries me still. In fact, it is one of the reasons why I have written this book. I hoped that in doing so I might find some clue which I had missed. But all that I have arrived at is a theory, which I will present when I have given the rest of the evidence for what it is worth.

Po Toke suspected that I did not intend to go back to Burma when the war was over. I did not welcome the prospects of post-war Burma and I had given the country twenty-five years of my life. I believe that just as the XIVth Army stood for Bombine, so Bombine stood for me in Po Toke's mind: and Po Toke knew he would see little of me for the rest of the war.

Whether that is so or not, after I had sacked him, Po Toke went back to Witok and in due course he got the two to three thousand rupees owing to him from the Bombine Provident Fund. On that he could have settled down and lived for the rest of his life had things become normal. But according to my informant, who went back to the chaos of those forests of Burma after the war was over, Po Toke did not settle down to a graceful, if modest, old age. With the money he got from Bombine he started a band of dacoits—perhaps he was enraged at the fact that the Burmese Government had nationalised all elephants—perhaps his hope for Burmese independence had gone sour on him, when he discovered so many of the members of the new Government were ex-Japanese collaborators—perhaps he'd always wanted to head a band of dacoits and only been restrained from doing so by the need to look after Bandoola—perhaps the failure of all the things in which he had believed had made him bitter. When one starts speculations of this sort, there is no end to them. All that is certain is that when all the forest assistants finally departed from Burma, Po Toke was one of the leaders of the dacoits making it difficult for any administration of New Burma.

I have always distrusted the statement that each man kills the thing he loves as being, if nothing else, too sweeping. But I suspect that it was true of Po Toke. The more I think of it, the more certain I am that his behaviour in the saw-mill camp was inconsistent with his innocence. Why should he lie about the length of time that Bandoola had been lost? Why, when he knew exactly where the carcase was, should he conceal the fact? Why, considering his hatred of Indians, should he not have reported the shooting instantly if an Indian had killed him?

Yet what could have induced Po Toke to kill the thing he loved? I have a theory, for which there is not a shred of evidence that would be accepted in a court of law, but which I think is probably true all the same.

I believe that working for the saw-mills for long hours, often indeed far into the night, Po Toke became desperate. If I had been there, he would have come to me and we would have worked out some arrangement as we had so often in the past. But I was far away, occupied with disposing of the thirty or forty tuskers which we were capturing from the Japanese each day. There wasn't a man to whom he could turn, who would understand what a truly remarkable elephant Bandoola was.

It is possible also that Po Toke had taken to smoking opium. I am not sure of that, but I am quite sure that he had gone slightly crazy during those nightmare six months he spent at Witok and that he never fully recovered. He was older than Bandoola; he would die before him. The only person to whom he might have trusted him was myself, and he had a shrewd suspicion that I would never go back.

So I think with a curious mixture of possessiveness and conceit ("No one can manage Bandoola like me") he took a service rifle and shot the animal he had defended and protected from birth. Then he sawed off one of the tusks to make it appear as if Bandoola had been killed for ivory and took this tusk as his memento.

Yet the very lack of consistency is what convinces me of the truth of my theory. For if I am right, this is one of the very few *crimes passionels* committed against an animal.

I don't know whether Po Toke is still alive; but if he is dead, I hope that he is celebrated by some other memorial than this book, if only as simple as that which was blazed upon a teak tree in the Kabaw valley.

EPILOGUE

THIS book may seem more complicated than *Elephant Bill*. There is the story of Po Toke and his two child-less wives and his one elephant Bandoola. There is the story of Elephant Bill and the discovery of contentment alone in the jungle and the even greater contentment of the jungle shared with one who is loved and loves the jungle. There are the stories of men, like Willie choosing the bottle before women yet keeping his eye in for the cricket tour on his home leave, and Millie reading the droppings of elephants like a book, of the brave and reckless Gerry Dawson and Kayem and the desperate Rasher. There are the stories of dogs like Ba Sein who saved my life and lost his own in a matter of days, and of Molly Mia who could hear me calling from five miles away. It seems, perhaps, as if this was all haphazard.

But I don't think that it really is. I have been trying to say in this book that I have found my happiness not in considering myself as Homo Sapiens set apart from the rest of creation, but in seeing that I fit in with the rest of nature, what are called so wrongly the animal and vegetable kingdoms. I believe that plants and animals have an immediate sensitiveness, an awareness of living, of what is good and what is perilous, that we humans cut ourselves off from to our own detriment. That is what the jungle has taught me.

Yet please do not think that I am a Buddhist. I would gladly exterminate all jungle leeches, the fungus which gives rise to elephant itch, the hookworm and innumerable other parasites. These are the enemy, not the bear, the tiger and the leopard, or wild elephants, for they are as ready to enter man's companionship as the South Devon bullocks grazing in front of me as I look up.

END